MW00624829

"Not only do we not know
God except through Jesus
Christ; We do not even know
ourselves except through
Jesus Christ."

— Blaise Pascal

author
Caesar Kalinowski
producer
Matt Smay
designer
Peter Schrock
editor
Hugh Halter and **bloomcreativellc.com**

Thanks from Caesar

The gospel is best understood and experienced through life in a community that is living in the grasp of the good news. It has been my privilege to be a part of Soma Communities and the many brothers and sisters that I live among on mission. It is within this community that the ideas and expressions of the gospel that are presented in this primer have been formed. I am forever grateful to God for all of you! Special thanks must go to my brother Jeff Vanderstelt for his understanding and gifting in helping us all live in and proclaim the gospel that transforms us!

All scripture quotations, unless otherwise indicated, are taken from the Holy Bible, New International Version®, NIV®. Copyright ©1973, 1978, 1984, 2011 by Biblica, Inc.™ Used by permission of Zondervan. All rights reserved worldwide. www.zondervan.com The "NIV" and "New International Version" are trademarks registered in the United States Patent and Trademark Office by Biblica, Inc.™

Scripture quotations from THE MESSAGE. Copyright © by Eugene H. Peterson 1993, 1994, 1995, 1996, 2000, 2001, 2002. Used by permission of NavPress Publishing Group.

Scripture quotations marked (NLT) are taken from the Holy Bible, New Living Translation, copyright © 1996, 2004, 2007 by Tyndale House Foundation. Used by permission of Tyndale House Publishers, Inc., Carol Stream, Illinois 60188. All rights reserved.

for more info or to find out about bulk discounts
www.missiopublishing.com

©2013 Missio Publishing
published by Missio Publishing
ISBN 978-0-9830864-6-8
Printed in China

THE
Gospel
primer

An eight-week guide to transformation in community

PREPARATION: Read this first!   vii

What Is The Gospel?   I
The Story   25
Your Gospel Story   49
Gospel Listening   73
Four Eternal Truths   97
Two Lenses   I2I
Gospel Identity   I45
Gospel Rhythms   I69

EPILOGUE AND APPENDIX   I93

Finally, after more than a decade of looking wistfully through catalogs, watching others experience the joy of the open road, and occasionally meandering through Harley shops around the country, my longings were fulfilled. In a jaw-dropping surprise for my 50th birthday, my son *gave* me a beautiful black and chrome Harley Davidson! Like a newborn baby, the bike was so beautiful that I took a bunch of photos on my smart-phone and sent it to all my friends. A proud man I was! Other men responded with *oohs* and *aahs*, expressing their desire to join me on the road with their own bikes.

It's been several months now, and because I live in Tacoma, I've only gotten to ride my bike a handful of times due to this pesky little thing in the northwest—rain! So, almost daily, I go outside to the garage to simply gaze at it. Don't get me wrong, I really enjoy looking at it, spit-shining the gas tank, wiping off the dust, and staring off into space trying to remember the few moments of bliss I've experienced. I imagine the wind in my face, the scent of pine trees, sea breezes, the camaraderie and joy of meeting fellow Harley riders in quaint little biker bars, the smell of my old leather jacket I brought out of retirement, and yes, the personal satisfaction of forgetting I'm now in my 50s and trying to look cool for my wife.

But just looking at my bike, or remembering past moments of glory, don't really do it for me. I want to ride again and hear the slow, sultry thug-thug of the engine. I want to smell the exhaust and feel the road beneath me again. Harleys are meant to be ridden; real life is meant to be lived. That's actually good news, man—really good news.

If you've gone through any of the Missio materials or heard any of us speak, you'll realize that our whole approach is to move you beyond concepts, small momentary experiences or memories of the past to actual life in God's kingdom.

The gospel proclaims that the kingdom is now among us and available to be lived in! This life, which can be experienced, enjoyed and offered to those around us, is like jumping on your first Harley. The kingdom will take you to new places, and mysteriously change the way you see everything. And that's why Jesus called it GOOD NEWS! The kingdom is about living, loving and leaving our purposeless and passionless quest for the American dream to whimsically follow Jesus on his great mission to transform the lives of people on every street in our cities and in every home in our neighborhoods.

But most of us settle for memories and mundane religion. We know things about the gospel, but we really don't know the GOSPEL.

If we're honest, most of us see very little change in our inner life or in our character. We continue to struggle with lusts of the flesh, with denying worldly temptations and concerns. We fight depression, fatigue, failed relationships with our kids and others. We are bound up in all sorts of anxieties and vices, and at the end of each day, we turn off the lights wondering if anything is changing us at the level of the soul.

As well, and as expected, we look upon God's mission as something only a few people get in on. We know we are God's ambassadors, his priests, and we understand that the church is supposed to be his missionaries in the world, but we just keep showing up to nebulous worship gatherings, empty Bible studies, or pathetic small groups.

Isn't there more? *I thought we were supposed to be "new creations"— what happened?!*

Having spent years pastoring people who are asking these same questions and feeling the ineffectiveness of applying more traditional "spiritual disciplines," I began to wonder how the apostles Paul and Peter, and the other disciples, managed to live such transformed lives—lives that were not only personally transformed, but that also changed the world. Don't get me wrong, I am in favor of, and have found great benefit in, many of the more traditional forms of spiritual discipline...time in the Word each day, prayer, keeping a journal, prayer-walking, etc. But those "disciplines" can easily leave you staring at your Harley instead of actually riding it! Starting with Jesus and his early disciples, people who have changed the world found a beautiful connection between spiritual disciplines and the vibrant life of God's spirit-led mission. They understood the real gospel.

We've called this resource a *primer* (which can be defined as a "book of basic principles"), but we do not assume that you are unfamiliar with the gospel. We do assume you may not be experiencing it and thus may not be aware of the fullness of the gospel. Perhaps it's time to revisit the central message and lifestyle that can truly change everything.

The *Gospel Primer* is about learning how the gospel of Jesus Christ transforms your identity and reshapes the very rhythms of your life. It is about becoming so familiar with the power and purpose of the gospel that it flows out of your life and words in normal, yet extraordinary ways. When the gospel increasingly transforms our life, perspectives and priorities, we *become* good news to everyone. We become a living proclamation and display of the God we love and his kingdom.

The Gospel Primer:
Where We're Going

You may be familiar with the *Tangible Kingdom Primer* and *Barefoot Church Primer*. Perhaps you've been part of a group that has gone through either or both of these primers together. If you have, the *Gospel Primer* is a great next step. If you are new to the *Missio Primer Series*, then this is the perfect place to start. Either way, getting grounded in your gospel identity and growing in gospel fluency will strengthen any group and provide the groundwork for a strong and vibrant missional community.

As we begin, we'll first provide a quick summary of some key concepts that you will need to understand in order to get everyone in your community on the same page. The first week of this *Gospel Primer* is pretty packed with content, but it is key to setting up the rest of our eight weeks together. Don't be intimidated. Jump in there!

We'd also like to share a few thoughts that will help you move beyond "just another Bible study group experience." Our intent is to provide a new framework for how you can live both naturally and intentionally to make the gospel of God's kingdom tangible to you and anyone you love.

We hope that, after finishing this eight-week guide, the new insights and habits will have become so ingrained in your heart and behavior that these missional rhythms become intuitive instead of programmed. Most small group guides assume that by completing the assignments you will accomplish the end goal of the small group. Our viewpoint is a little different. We hope that at the end of the eight weeks, you will have successfully begun the journey, not finished it.

So, in this case, the end is just the beginning! At the end of these next eight weeks we would love to help you and your community take what you have learned and go to the next level of intentionality; moving even further into forming communities that work to make disciples within a very specific and defined context of people. Keep this in mind as you wrestle through each day and adjust your expectations accordingly.

The Gospel Primer:
Basic Concepts

We've tried to use language in this primer that is clear and understandable to everyone no matter if you grew up going to Sunday school every week or if you've never attended a single church service. But before we get started, there are a few special terms that we want to make sure are clear.

Apprenticeship
Moving beyond knowledge-based discipleship to action-oriented followership, with the goal of living like Jesus lived. This comes through regular practice, faith-oriented action, and personal devotion to know the ways of Christ.

The Gospel
The news that God has entered the world in Jesus Christ to achieve a salvation that we could not achieve for ourselves. The good news of Jesus is capable of transforming everything about a person, their community, and their world.

Gospeling
The word gospel used as a verb (in an action sense) to mean we are applying the truth of the gospel to a person, our own hearts or a specific situation (i.e., she gospeled my heart concerning my job loss).

Gospel Fluency
Our ability to speak and display the gospel in natural and effective ways in any situation in life, leading to transformation and restoration.

Gospel Identity
The fullness of who God has made us in Christ when we put our hope and trust in him for our salvation.

Gospel Listening
The ability to listen through the framework of the gospel as others speak, gaining an understanding of what is specifically "good news" to an individual.

Rhythms
Patterns and habits of life that are common to everyone in every culture and context.

The 4 G's
Four eternal truths about God's character that never change: God is great, glorious, good and gracious. Unbelief in any of these areas leads us into sin.

The Intuitive Life

Our choices, motives and decisions now led by the Holy Spirit. A Spirit-empowered lifestyle guided by a capacity to sense and respond to God's direction.

The Gospel Primer:
The Weekly Rhythm

Incarnational community is the framework of life in which God has called us all to live. It's the best context for our spiritual growth. It will provide the most natural way to enlarge the gospel picture for your friends who are seeking God right now. But as we said, it doesn't just happen on its own.

We're going to provide an initial pathway that will help you and your community deal with the inner-life challenges to understanding the gospel and living on mission. We'll also give you some intentional activities and reflections that we have found helpful for us. To do this, you'll notice that the primer is set up in a daily format for each person to complete individually. We suggest spending about 20-30 minutes a day on this. As with any spiritual formation practice, we highly recommend you take those times seriously. Take time to get in a quiet, undistracted space, breathe, begin with silence, then invite God to speak. Read every word slowly and fight the urge to move too quickly. Every question has a purpose. Every scripture is the breath of God. If you ask God to direct your thoughts and writing, HE WILL. If you just buzz through it, you'll miss him.

Although we're following what appears to be a highly structured process, we all know that life doesn't always work like this. Our hope is that the structure we're creating of seven daily practices and reflections will help you begin to understand and incorporate the key components of personal and communal renewal into your life.

Day 1: EXPLORATION

The first day of the weekly rhythm will introduce you to the subject of the week and provide thoughts, stories, and definitions to help you get an understanding of the concepts. We'll also provide questions and journaling space so that you can wrestle with what this stuff means in your life and in the life of your community. And here's fair warning: we've intentionally written questions that we hope will challenge you. They may even make you uncomfortable sometimes. We look at it this way—we can make these eight weeks easy and somewhat pointless, or we can make room for the gospel to get in deep where it can make a difference. The good news is that if you let it, it will change your life. And that's what we're after.

It often helps, on this first day, to take a quick look at your Action Day and Community Day in order to be fully prepared.

Day 2: MEDITATION

On Day 2, we'll provide you with a scripture or two to soak in for a little while. Read it a couple times and let it do its work in you. Don't forget the questions on the next page.

Day 3: CHANGE

The Change Day is where we start to get serious. What does this idea mean in your life? How would your life be different if you began to let it be changed by the gospel? There are questions for journaling on this day as well.

Day 4: ACTION

By now you've begun to let your heart be changed; how about your hands and feet? Action Day is about putting it into practice. As we work our way through these eight weeks, we'll give you tasks to do. It's absolutely critical that you follow through with these assignments. The success of your group and your personal growth will depend on it.

Day 5: COMMUNITY

This day is meant to be a model for how our lives in community are to be increasingly lived out. This is a day when you get together with the other members of your community (those other folks who are putting this stuff into practice along with you) and do something together. Plan to have a simple meal together each of these Community Days. In our opinion, this and the Action Day are the most important day of the week. In fact, this whole process is going to be really difficult unless you do it with a few friends. Healthy community on mission (with God and with each other) is at the center of all that we're talking about.

Day 6: CALIBRATION

On Day 6, we'll revisit the theme of the week from a different angle and give you some additional things to think about as you wrestle with the topic of the week, allowing God to bring transformation into your life.

Day 7: RECREATE

The last day of our cycle should include times of rest and reflect a heart of Sabbath. This is a reminder to each of us that taking a break is a biblical pattern, one we like to call ReCreate: we rest in Jesus' completed work on our behalf, and out of that rest we create value, beauty, work. Not to earn God's approval, but creating/working out of the rest we have in Christ.

We intentionally keep Day 7 simple so you can save time for listening. We tend to keep so busy that we couldn't hear from God if he was shouting at us. And he rarely shouts. Try hard not to rush. Stop for a little while and listen.

Putting a Group Together

We have learned that it helps to give people time to process the tough inner life issues individually and then come together. Before you begin the process, pick a day your community will initially begin to meet. Ultimately the goal is to increasingly begin to live like a family on God's mission together throughout the week—a people who can see and apply how the gospel affects all of life. What may start out as a weekly meeting, or feel like baby steps, will grow into a lifestyle and increased gospel fluency with your identity rooted in Christ.

As we've already mentioned, we suggest you do this with a group of close friends. You can present the idea to a group you are already a part of: a missional community, house church, small group or Bible study. Or you can invite some friends to join you in creating a new community. How ever this group is made up or

formed, there doesn't necessarily have to be any initial commitment beyond getting together weekly for the next eight weeks to
explore these ideas together.

While there are no limitations on the number of people in your
initial community, we have found that somewhere between the 6
and 12 range is usually a good place to start. Typically, a group this
size can easily fit in most homes or an apartment, is large enough
to accommodate the occasional absentee, and is small enough
not to require a master coordinator to facilitate meals together.
The group can include mature believers, new Christ followers and
sojourners that may not be sure about their beliefs. The *Gospel
Primer* is a perfect place to start!

Remember, the actual mission Jesus sends his followers on is
a disciple-making mission. These communities are ultimately
going to be about helping yourself and others increasingly walk
in Jesus' ways as you grow in your identity in Christ and apply the
gospel to every area of your life.

What is the Gospel?

EXPLORATION

A few years ago I was with a group of Christians, many of them pastors and leaders, and I asked them the question, "What is the gospel?" I waited for their response. I assumed that such a simple and obviously important question would net immediate and similar answers from everyone. Boy was I wrong!

I heard a dozen completely different answers and not one of them mentioned creation, sin, Jesus, the cross, or the kingdom. How could this be? And if a bunch of pastors could not give a good answer to this question, it made me wonder what kind of gospel message would be coming from the lips of the people they lead and serve?

So what is the Gospel?

The gospel is called the "good news" and it is particularly good news concerning our relationship with God.

In a nutshell, we can sum it up this way: *The gospel is that God himself has come to rescue and renew creation in and through the work of Jesus Christ on our behalf.*[1] Why does creation (which includes you and me) need rescuing? Because of sin.

This may sound heavy at first, but it's the truth. In order to understand the good news, we really do need to have a right understanding of sin. God is not focused on our sin, but it is what has broken our relationship with him and messed up our true identity.

Sin is making everything about ME. Sin is living life my way, for my fame and glory, instead of living God's way for God. We have all sinned and really need the gospel—we desperately need Jesus to rescue us from the penalty and effects of our sin.

When we repent (change our mind about who is really God in our lives) and by faith believe that Jesus' life, death and resurrection has restored us to a right relationship with God the Father, then this good news begins to change every area of our life back to the way God designed it to be.

Becoming Gospel Fluent

In order to effectively equip our missional community to be "fluent" in the gospel, we will need to create a culture where it is normal to speak the gospel to each other regularly, naturally.

Every sin and issue that stands in the way of our faithfulness to God's design and Jesus' commands is ultimately a gospel issue. Since all sin is the outcome of unbelief in God, we can learn to apply the truth about him and the good news to every area of our lives. To do this, we will have to learn to trust God and others with our sin and the messiness of our lives.

*See to it, brothers and sisters, that none of you has a sinful, **unbelieving heart** that turns away from the living God.* [Hebrews 3:12]

The foundation of a gospel-centered, missional life is the decision to offer to God our plans in exchange for his plans. We must allow the truth about who God is, what he has done, and our new identity in Christ to inform all of life.

God himself
has come to
rescue and renew
all creation
through the work of Jesus.

1.1 Notes

While visiting the Czech Republic many times over the past ten years, I have learned little bits of their language. But when I try to speak I end up sounding more like a caveman uttering mispronounced words, ideas and comments in short, stunted bursts of uncertainty. The looks on their kind Czech faces confirm my fears: they have very little idea what I am talking about! Not good.

I wonder if that is how we often sound to each other and those who are not-yet believers when we speak about Jesus and his kingdom? How fluent in the gospel are you?

If someone you know were to ask you the question, "What is the gospel?" how would you answer them? Write down your answer.

What has usually been the response from people you have shared the gospel with in the past?

Does your gospel truly sound like "good news" to people? (If so, they would really want to hear it...)

In the past, what has kept you from regularly sharing and applying the gospel with people more often? Circle all that apply:

Fear / Clarity / Pride / Unbelief / Apathy
Too busy / Might damage relationship / Disobedience

How "fluent" in speaking and applying the gospel are you? On a scale of 1-10 where would you rate your current fluency and abilities today?

.2
MEDITATION

Speaking the truth in love, we will grow to become in every respect the mature body of him who is the head, that is, Christ.

Jesus answered, "I am the way and the truth and the life."

Jesus is the

Encourage one another and build each other up.

It is written: "I believed; therefore I have spoken." Since we have that same spirit of faith, we also believe and therefore speak.

Therefore encourage one another daily, as long as it is called "Today," so that none of you may be hardened by sin's deceitfulness.

Good News.

Speaking the truth in love is how we are built up and matured into greater Christ-likeness. Jesus is the truth. Jesus is the gospel. The good news about Jesus' life death and resurrection is not just a set of historical facts; it is good news in context—specifically—about every area in our life. We need to "preach the gospel" to our own hearts, and others we love, regularly rehearsing what is true because of Jesus.

Read more: Ephesians 4:15-16, John 14:6, Hebrews 3:13,
2 Corinthians 4:13, 1 Thessalonians 5:11

1.2 Notes

Think about all the many things that were accomplished on your behalf by Jesus' perfect life, his death and resurrection...this is all VERY good news! Look up each of these verses and write down what is now true because of Jesus' life, death and resurrection.

Reference	What is Now True Because of Jesus?
John 5:24	
2 Corinthians 5:17	
Romans 5:1	
Romans 8:1	
Romans 8:2	

Ephesians 1:5

Ephesians 3:16-18

Colossians 3:1-4

1 John 4:7-12

Revelation 12:10,11

Jesus' life and teaching always attracted a crowd; he was loved by the irreligious and was outcast and hated by the moralistic, legalistic religious types. If our lives and proclamation of the gospel are not having a similar effect in our culture, then it is probably a different message we proclaim.

CHANGE

The gospel has saved us from the penalty of sin.
The gospel is saving us from the power of sin.
The gospel will save us from the presence of sin.
The gospel did not just happen...it is HAPPENING!

When I first "got saved" my understanding of the gospel was pretty much focused on getting out of hell and where I would spend my afterlife. And it is true, when I accepted Jesus' death in place of my own, my sins were forgiven and I inherited eternal life with God.

But I thought little about the reality that because of his death and resurrection, Jesus enables me to say "no" to the power and pull of sin in my life NOW, beginning to live the life I was created to live. And there is a day coming when Jesus returns to put away all sin and sickness and destruction. Everything will be restored to the way God originally created it. The gospel is a past, present and future reality.

Something to think about:
"The gospel of Christ is inherently a missionary gospel. It is a message that changes a life, changes a course, changes affections, changes values, changes worldview, changes love, changes loyalty, and should change either our giving or our going—or both. But the gospel cannot leave you as you are, the way you are, and where you are, or it cannot possibly be the gospel you have received." [Kevin Turner]

"Entering into this fullness is not something you figure out or achieve. It's not a matter of being circumcised or keeping a long list of laws. No, you're already in—insiders—not through some secretive initiation rite but rather through what Christ has already gone through for you, destroying the power of sin. If it's an initiation ritual you're after, you've already been through it by submitting to baptism. Going under the water was a burial of your old life; coming up out of it was a resur- rection, God raising you from the dead as he did Christ. When you were stuck in your old sin-dead life, you were incapable of responding to God. God brought you alive—right along with Christ! Think of it! All sins forgiven, the slate wiped clean, that old arrest warrant canceled and nailed to Christ's cross. He stripped all the spiritual tyrants in the universe of their sham authority at the cross and marched them naked through the streets." [Colossians 2:11-15 The Message]

1.3 Notes

Which of your past sins were dealt with at the cross? Which of your present and future sins were forgiven too?

What shifts in your heart and life when you think about the gospel as a past, present, and future reality?

How does this change the way you view your sin?

How does this reality effect your current relationship with God? With others?

1.4
ACTION

salvation
justification
adoption
sanctification

Speak Gospel Truths

When we intentionally speak the gospel to others, it is often helpful to think about and speak one or more of these four aspects of the gospel: salvation, justification, adoption, and sanctification. Here is a paraphrase...

Because of the perfect life, sacrificial death and eternal resurrection of Jesus, we are...

*Completely saved from the penalty of our sin, given a more abundant life now, and eternal life with God. That's **salvation.***

*Declared right with God because of Jesus' perfect life exchanged for ours. That's **justification.***

*Children fully loved and accepted by our Father, made part of his forever family. That's **adoption**.*

*Becoming more like Jesus as we begin to live out what is now true of us in the power of the Holy Spirit. That's **sanctification.***

Speak Gospel Implications

So as we think of these gospel truths, it helps us speak the corresponding implications directly into each other's lives. It helps
to remind us of how the gospel works transformation and Jesus'
mission into our lives. Here are a few of the implications for
each of these.

Because of the gospel, we...

*Do not have to live with guilt or shame over our past sins or present
areas of our life that God is still working on. We have been given a
totally new life in Christ! Therefore, we can extend forgiveness and
grace to others with great courage and flexibility.* **This is salvation.**

*Do not need to control others' opinions of us or try to impress God
with our spirituality since the Father now sees Jesus' perfect life and
status when he looks at us. Therefore, we can live with deep humility, yet much gratitude, confidence and joy.* **This is justification.**

*Have nothing to earn because we're already fully loved, approved
and valued by our Father. Therefore, we can love and serve all people, even our enemies, with no strings attached.* **This is adoption.**

*Do not need to look to anything else for identity and purpose since
we have been reborn by the Holy Spirit. Therefore, we can re-orient
our whole lives around the mission of Jesus to make disciples.* **This
is sanctification.**

GET STARTED
Take a walk somewhere quiet where you can think and listen
to God speak. Pick at least two of these gospel truths (or go for
all four) and apply them to your life, past and present. Which of
these gives you the most peace?

1.5
COMMUNITY

Hanging Out Around the Gospel

Meet at a group member's home or some other place where you can share a meal together and talk.

Wow...we got started fast! Maybe your view of the gospel is already changing considerably. Take some time tonight to share some of the "lightbulbs" that might have come on.

Discuss these questions together...

How has the gospel gotten bigger in your understanding?

Did any of you have an "Aha!" moment with God this week?

What shifted for you?

How should the gospel implications affect our lives individually?

How would it affect us as a community?

How would that affect others...our neighborhood, our city?

1.6
CALIBRATION

angelism = Discipleship = Evangelism = Discipleship = Evangelism
Discipleship = Evangelism = Discipleship = Evangelism = Disci
scipleship = Evangelism = Discipleship = Evangelism = Discipleship
Evangelism = Discipleship = Evangelism = Discipleship = Evang
angelism = Discipleship = Evangelism = Discipleship = Evangelism
Discipleship = Evangelism = Discipleship = Evangelism = Disci
scipleship = Evangelism = Discipleship = Evangelism = Discipleship
vangelism = Discipleship = Evangelism = Discipleship = Evangeli

For many of us, evangelism is what happens to bring us (or others) to the point of belief. In contrast, we usually understand discipleship as the process for growth in our Christian life. Evangelism "gets us in the door" and then the work of discipleship begins.

But let's look a little closer. The word *evangel* means "gospel." And *to evangelize* means "to preach the gospel." In the same way that we come to put our faith in Jesus by hearing and experiencing the gospel, we also continue to grow and mature by the light of that same gospel. This is a lifelong process. We are *always* in need of evangelism. In fact, discipleship can be simply understood as the ongoing "evangelizing" of our hearts.

Jesus described it this way. He said, "If you hold to my teaching, you are really my disciples." Clear and simple. And then he went on to say something really interesting: "Then you will know the truth, and the truth will set you free" (John 8:31-32). In Jesus's view, the whole thing starts with learning to follow him, becoming his disciples. As we enter that process, and as a result of it, our lives are transformed and we are set free from guilt, shame and the weight of sin. This is what discipleship is all about! According to Jesus, we are discipled to the truth that sets us free.

Evangelism = Discipleship = Evangelism = Discipleship = Evangelism = Discipleship = Evangelism = Discipleship = Evangelism = Discipleship = Evangelism = Discipleship = Evangelism = Discipleship = Evangelism = Discipleship = Evangelism = Discipleship = Evangelism = Discipleship = Evangelism = Discipleship = Evangelism = Discipleship = Evangelism = Discipleship = Evangelism = Discipleship = Evangelism = Discipleship = Evangelism = Discipleship = Evangelism = Discipleship

So we see that whether we are talking about our own hearts or the hearts and lives of our friends and neighbors, the process of discipleship (evangelism in its truest sense) can begin long before a confession of faith and continue throughout our entire lives. This is what it means to say that the gospel saves and sanctifies us.

1.6 Notes

From what you've learned this week, what is the hardest part of the good news for you to believe personally?

What areas of your life do you most need to apply the gospel to? Can you see more clearly how your own discipleship is connected closely to regularly being reminded of what is true in Christ?

Who are one or two other people you could regularly (weekly) get together with to gospel one another's hearts? Take the initiative by inviting them to get started soon.

In what ways have you moved from faith in Jesus' work on your behalf to your own hard work and discipline in your Christian life? (Check out Galatians 3:1-14)

I.7
ReCREATE

We'll wrap up each week with a challenge to remain intentionally restful. This day should remind you of the biblical pattern of Sabbath.

While today may not be a day you can fully set aside to rest, you might have another day of the week where you can make some space for rest. If so, include the ideas and thoughts from Day 7 into your regular weekly day of rest, whenever it is. We find it helpful to think of this rhythm as ReCreate: we rest in Jesus and out of that rest we create value, beauty, work and serve others.

There was a group of early Christians in a city called Galatia that had come to put their faith in Jesus, but then had tried to grow and mature by hard work and observing religious laws and ceremony. The apostle Paul has a few things to say to them...and to us:

"Oh, foolish Galatians! Who has cast an evil spell on you? For the meaning of Jesus Christ's death was made as clear to you as if you had seen a picture of his death on the cross. Let me ask you this one question: Did you receive the Holy Spirit by obeying the law of Moses? Of course not! You received the Spirit because you believed the message you heard about Christ. How foolish can you be? After starting your Christian lives in the Spirit, why are you now trying to become perfect by your own human effort? Have you experienced so much for nothing? Surely it was not in vain, was it?"

[Galatians 3:1-4 NLT]

Consider praying this prayer...

Father, thank you for the gospel, thank you that your son Jesus. Forgive me for not trusting you with my soul, and for not trusting you in so many areas of my life, today. Please help me, by your own Spirit, to rest in Jesus's completed work on the cross, trusting you with my past, with my present and with my future. **Amen.**

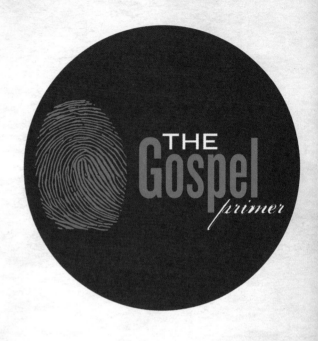

WEEK 2
The Story

2.1
EXPLORATION

Our lives are wrapped up in stories. They are the language of our world. Think about your favorite movies or books. They draw you in... you begin to feel what the characters feel... their pain becomes your pain... their victory becomes your victory. We enter the drama and it becomes part of our own experience. Stories are the most powerful form of communication we have; they speak to the mind, the body and the emotions.

Everyone has a story
and all people are storytellers.

I grew up going to Sunday school pretty much every week of my young life. Our teachers told us amazing stories from the Bible, all of them ending with a nice moral like, *"If you had faith like David you could slay any 'giant' in your own life too!"* Or, *"So kids, if you are obedient like Noah, God will protect you from all the bad stuff in your life too."*

Not only did they often miss the point of the narrative (God is always the hero!), but they never taught us that the Bible is one BIG story. In fact, **it is the gospel Story.** It's not a collection of unrelated moralistic tales, nor is it a history lesson. The Bible tells a living and active story that is STILL happening, and we are part of the adventure!

Identity:
Who we believe ourselves to be is shaped by the dominant story in our life.

We live in story, and all of us have been shaped by a dominant story. Is the story that most shapes your life and identity the story of God that is told throughout the Bible? Or is it a story from your culture, dysfunctional background or a stack of lies that makes up the primary narrative of your life? What we believe about God and what he is like will ultimately determine what we believe about ourselves and how life works.

Part of our gospel fluency comes from a clear understanding of the story of God and our ability to simply yet powerfully relate this story to circumstances in our life and the lives of others. We learn to find our place in, and see how our lives intersect with, God's big story. We can learn to tell God's story naturally and comfortably, like a servant, sharing a story so powerful that it changes lives!

2.1 Notes

How would your view of yourself (and your life) change if the story of God found in the Bible is still going on...and it includes YOU?!

Who do you view yourself to be? What makes up your identity? (roles, relationships, family, abilities, talents, occupation?) Make a list.

Be honest...which of these aspects of your identity gives you your greatest dose of self worth and value?

What would you include if you were to tell a concise, yet complete, version of God's story to an unbelieving friend or neighbor if asked to?

2.2

THE STORY OF GOD

CREATION \ FALL \ REDEMPTION \ RESTORATION

This is a story found in the Bible, about God, a being who has always existed and is the creator of everything. God is the only one in this story who always does what is good, right and perfect—the Bible calls him holy. While God created the foundations of the earth, angels (his first creation) were there watching. They sang together and worshiped God... but some of these angels rebelled against God and his ways. The Bible teaches that all rebellion against God is called sin. And because of God's holiness he will not allow sin to remain in his presence, so he sent the rebellious angels, now known as demons, down into darkness on the earth.

Then God decided to create other beings, called humans, in his own image. God said, "Let us make man in our image to be like us." He then prepared the earth as a place for the humans to live—filling the earth with plants, birds, fish and animals of all kinds. God created the first humans, Adam and Eve, and placed them in a beautiful garden and trusted them to care for and rule over all of his creation on earth. He told them, "be fruitful and multiply."

Daily, God would come and spend time with the humans, walking with them in the cool of the day. He showed them how to live in the best possible way—a life lived close to God and under his protection—a life that is full and complete and eternal. God looked at all that he had created and saw that it was very good!

Unfortunately, Adam and Eve eventually chose to rebel against God and his authority, choosing to live in their own ways instead of his. Since God will not allow evil and rebellion to remain in his presence, Adam and Eve were sent out of the garden, away from God. Separated from God and no longer following his ways, they were now subject to sickness, pain, and death. God told them, "The way you have chosen to live will bring you great struggles and pain, and then you will return to the ground from which you came." Not only were these humans now separated from God because of their sin, but they would also suffer death as they were separated from the Giver of Life.

After leaving the garden, the number of humans on earth grew rapidly. Sin spread from Adam and Eve to their sons and it continued to spread from generation to generation. Even though humans were created in God's image, everyone chose to disobey God. They all constantly acted out in violence against each other. This went on for thousands of years.

Then God established a special relationship and a covenant promise—representing the deepest of all agreements—with a man named Abraham. God told Abraham, "I'll make you the father of a great nation and famous throughout history. I will bless those who bless you and curse those who curse you. The entire earth will be blessed through your descendants. I will always be your God and you will always be my people."

Abraham's family, called the Israelites, were to be a new kind of people who would show the world what it means to once again live in God's ways. God gave them a vast amount of land where they enjoyed his blessings as they grew into a large nation.

But as time went by, the Israelites began doing what was right in their own eyes and rebelled against God and his laws. They stopped trusting in God and worshiped idols—people, things, wealth and power—over God. In their rebellion, the Israelites faced great struggles and ended up a defeated nation of slaves. But God continued to love his people and promised that one day one of their descendents would come to rescue and restore humanity, and all of creation, back to the way God originally created it.

Then there were 400 years of silence between God and his people.

The Israelites, called Jews, had been under the control of other nations for hundred of years. They were now ruled by Rome, the most powerful empire the world had ever known.

Finally, God sent an angel to a young woman named Mary in the town of Nazareth. The angel appeared to her and said, "You will become pregnant and have a son, and you are to name him Jesus. He will become a king whose kingdom will never end! This will happen supernaturally by God's Spirit, so this baby will be called God's Son."

God revealed to Mary and her soon-to-be-husband Joseph that this boy was the long awaited Messiah King, the one whom God promised he'd send to rescue his people! Sure enough, the next year Mary gave birth to a son whom she named Jesus, which means "the God who saves." Jesus grew up in both height and wisdom, and was loved by God and everyone who knew him. He lived a remarkable life, always choosing to live in God's ways and do what was good, right and perfect.

As a man, Jesus called people to follow him, inviting them to be a part of what he called the kingdom of God, calling people to once again live under God's rule and reign. He said, "God blesses those who realize their need for him; the humble and poor, the gentle and merciful—the kingdom of God belongs to them. God blesses the pure in heart and those who hunger and thirst to be with him." He taught people that the kingdom of God is within our hearts.

He said, "God showed his great love for people by sending me—his only son—to this world. Anyone

who believes in me and lives in my ways will find life that is complete and eternal! He sent me here to save people—not to judge them. Those who want to live in sin and darkness will reject me and bring God's judgment on themselves. But those who want to live in God's ways will trust me and live forever!"

As God had promised, he sent Jesus to rescue humanity from sin and the penalty of death. God accepted Jesus' perfect life in place of our own. Jesus was brutally beaten and died painfully on a wooden cross, taking the punishment that all of rebellious humanity deserved! Three days later Jesus conquered death when God raised him back to life and he was seen by over 500 eyewitnesses.

Soon afterward, Jesus went to be with his Father in heaven, rising up into the clouds right before his followers' eyes! He promised that he would send his own Holy Spirit to come and dwell within them. The Spirit would remind them of all Jesus taught, transform their hearts to be like Jesus and give them power to walk in the ways of God like Jesus did. Jesus also sent his followers to go out and tell others about him—his life and his sacrifice for their sins—and lead them to trust him and walk in his ways.

This was the beginning of what the Bible calls the Church—a community of people all over the world who, because of Jesus, once again enjoy a life that is full and complete—living in the ways of God.

We can join this amazing story... the story continues with us!

The Bible also tells us the end of this story... Jesus promised to come back one day to destroy all evil, sin and rebellion. Then there will be no more sickness, pain, or death. God's kingdom will come in fullness, and everyone and everything will live under his rule. Until then, we get to live in God's ways, giving people a foretaste of what life is like in the kingdom.

2.2 Notes

What sticks out to you after reading this short summary narrative of the story of God?

What do you wonder about after reading the story?

What did you learn about God from this? What did you learn about Jesus? Take some time to consider the patterns that show up throughout the story.

Do you think that most people you know have heard and understood this basic, yet powerful story? Is this the dominant cultural understanding of who God and Jesus are? How do you think that most people view the Bible?

What would change if more and more people had the opportunity to listen to and engage God's story in meaningful ways in a safe, shared environment?

Pray and ask God who he would want you to share his story with. and then get ready...write down the names of at least two friends (they might even be sojourners) that you could practice sharing this story with, from memory, later this week.

2.3

CHANGE

Our Human Job Description

On the first day of this week, we talked a little bit about the things that make up our identity–who we see ourselves to be. Most of us have carefully built an identity from the things we do and the roles that we fulfill, projecting a certain image of ourselves to others.

But we have seen in God's story that the most important thing about any of us is that we were created in the image of God. Crazy really... and God called that "very good!"

Adam and Eve did not have to do anything to earn or prove their identity. They were created in God's image, to be like him, and God declared them very good.

Every human being you have ever laid eyes on (including yourself in the mirror) has been created in God's image. Even though our sin and rebellion has marred that image, it never gets completely covered up or destroyed. It does not depend on us to obtain or maintain God's image in us. It is his job and his desire. That's why he sent Jesus to save and restore us—and ultimately all things—to the way he created us to be.

Humans have always wondered, *"What is the meaning of life...why am I here?"* If we were to boil it down to its simplest form, we see that we were made to 1) display God's image, 2) live in a close relationship with him, and 3) care for his creation, including people.

This is what I like to call our **human job description.** Pretty simple. Pretty cool.

The truth is, God initiated all of this in us, and it is God, through his indwelling Spirit that now empowers us to live this out. Jesus' death on the cross washed away our sin problem allowing us to better display what God is like. It is God who pursues an eternal relationship with us. It is only through God's love for us that we truly love and care for others in a way that accurately reflects his love and care for the entire world.

Our true identity is rooted in who God is, and what he is like. When we live out of that identity, displaying what is true of us because it is true of him, this is our greatest act of worship!

1 *Display God's image*

2 *Live in a close relationship with him*

3 *Care for his creation, including people*

2.3 Notes

What would change in your life if your true identity was not based on what you did - a role you play - but instead was based solely on being created in the image of God?

If this story does not center on us (but on God), how do/should we find our purpose in life?

God tells the first humans to be fruitful and multiply. In light of our "human job description," do you feel fruitful? If not, what stands in the way? (Think about how you invest your time, talents, money, career, etc.)

What does it mean to be fruitful?

To make this more personal, who would benefit from you bearing more fruit? Write their names down here.

2.4
ACTION

"Stories are the most prominent biblical way of helping us see ourselves in 'the God story,' which always gets around to the story of God making and saving us."

"Stories, in contrast to abstract statements of truth, tease us into becoming participants in what is being said."

"We find ourselves involved in the action. We may start as spectators or critics, but if the story is good (and the biblical stories are very good!), we find ourselves no longer just listening to but inhabiting the story."

- Eugene H. Peterson

Tell the story of God, from memory, as best you can to one or two people today. Try and do this over a meal or a cup of coffee. Remember, it is through practice that we grow in natural confidence, ability and fluency. First read through the story a few more times to lodge it deeper into your heart and memory.

Remember, it is the Spirit that makes God's story true for us, and true to others; it is his work, not our perfect telling of the story that makes it good news.

Ideas for telling God's story

- ▶ Tell a friend at work that you're trying to learn how to tell a story well and wondered if you could practice on them
- ▶ Tell the story at dinner to your family
- ▶ Practice telling the story to another person from your group that is going through the primer with you
- ▶ Tell the story to your spouse or a close friend

After telling the story, ask a few questions like these...

- ▶ Did this story make sense to you?
- ▶ What sticks out to you after hearing the story?
- ▶ What do you wonder about after hearing this?
- ▶ What did you learn about God from the story?

2.5
COMMUNITY

Make a list of 5 to 7 things you learned about God from the story.

QUESTIONS FOR DISCUSSION

Which parts of the story of God are most relevant in your own life today. Why? What parts of it most remind you of your own story?

Take turns sharing about who you practiced telling the story with yesterday and how it went.

Discuss what you learned from telling the story.

Pray together asking God to show each of you people in your life that do not know the story of God... someone that God would have you, in the future, spend more time with and tell his story to. Pray about how you might do this together in community.

Note: A simple yet powerful way that many missional communities have grown in their knowledge and understanding of the gospel is by going through *The Story-formed Way* together. Go to **http://www.gcmcollective. org/article/story-formed-way** for a free download of this great resource.

2.6
CALIBRATION

One of the recurring themes we see in the story is how God pursues a relationship with the people he has created. He walked in the cool of the day with Adam and Eve, and as soon as they rebelled, he went looking for them (Genesis 3:8,9).

We saw God pursue a relationship with Abraham and his descendants, Israel, desiring them to be his own chosen people—his earthly family. God even moved into a tent and hung out with the Israelites for decades! (Exodus 25:8,9)

But God desired to be even closer to his beloved image-bearers. He sent his son Jesus to restore our broken relationship, actually taking on flesh and dwelling among us!

The names given Jesus at his birth tell us a lot about who he is and why he came; the name Jesus means, "the Lord saves." Emmanuel means, "God with us." Jesus came to be with us and to save us—to restore us to a right relationship with his Father.

After his death and resurrection, Jesus told his disciples that it was good that he was going away so that he could send his own Spirit to come and dwell inside of them!

So God got even closer to us by coming and making his home inside of us. We are now his tent, his temple, his body! Because of Jesus, we can enjoy a relationship with God that is closer than we ever thought imaginable.

"The Spirit of God, who raised Jesus from the dead, lives in you. And just as God raised Christ Jesus from the dead, he will give life to your mortal bodies by this same Spirit living within you."

[Romans 8:11]

2.6 Notes

Think about things you did to pursue a relationship with someone you had a crush on? How does it make you feel that God has pursued you your entire life, desiring a relationship with you?

How does the story of God shape how you believe God thinks about you?

What parts of your own personal story is God still pursuing and wanting to restore?

What have you learned about your true identity from God's story?

What are some first steps to begin to be the "hands and feet" of Jesus and begin to live out his pursuit for others as a way of life?

2.7
ReCREATE

Then the man and his wife heard the sound of the LORD God as he was walking in the garden in the cool of the day, and they hid from the LORD God among the trees of the garden (Genesis 3:8). So I say, walk by the Spirit, and you will not gratify the desires of the flesh (Galatians 5:16). For in him we live and move and have our being (Acts 17:28).

Consider this...

After rebelling against God and his ways, Adam and Eve hid from God. Their sin filled them with shame. But there is good news for us! Because of Jesus, we can now live un-ashamed lives that beautifully display what God is like and who he has made us to be. Our stories have been redeemed. Cleansed from sin, we are now indwelled by the Holy Spirit who leads and guides us.

Today, rest in the knowledge that God still wants to walk with you in the cool of the day!

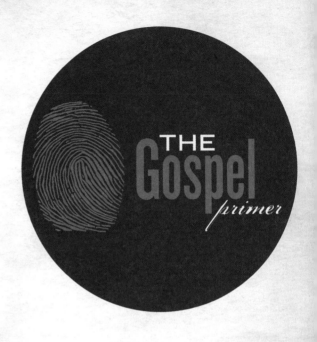

WEEK 3

Your Gospel Story

Creation

Fall

Redemption

Restoration

God is the Hero

My favorite singers, songwriters, comedians, preachers or public speakers all have one thing in common: they know how to tell a good story. When they finish telling a story I feel connected to it—and them—in some profound way. I can relate in laughter or tears, in agreement or disagreement, but I connect powerfully with the stories they tell.

That's how it works in the rest of our lives too. We get to know each other and build friendships by sharing our stories. We are bound together by common themes and the things we have jointly experienced. In fact that is how relationship and community happens...our common stories connect us, bind us together.

Deep down inside, even if we can't explain it, we all yearn to be connected to something bigger. That is because our lives are all actually part of a much, much larger story. Last week, we focused on the one dominant story that we all find our lives connected to. God's story comes before, finishes, corrects and ultimately makes sense of all other stories.

In order to effectively share the gospel with people, we must learn how to tell our stories through the lens of the larger story: Creation ➡ Fall ➡ Redemption ➡ Restoration.

Unfortunately, when we tell our story, we often like to make ourselves the center of attention, the star of the show. And if we *do* mention God in our story, it's likely just to make ourselves sound "spiritual". Most of the time, we look pretty good and while God plays the role of a helpful sidekick, we are the primary focus—the hero—in our story.

However, there's a better, more truthful way. We can learn to tell our stories in a way that glorifies God and is both challenging and inspiring to others. Our stories can be salty like potato chips — no one can eat just one! — and be light that illuminates a path toward new life in the kingdom.

3.1 Notes

In the past, how have you told your story, or "given your testimony"? How often do you tell this story? Does it seem natural to others who hear it? What has been their response?

If you have a written version of your story/testimony take it out and re-read it. Who is the hero of the story? If it is God, that's great! If it is you or someone/something else, why?

When in your life have you seen the greatest intersections between God's story and your story?

When in your life have you most consistently turned to God for help and relationship? What was happening?

What was happening in your life when you felt furthest from God?

3.2

MEDITATION

For you created my inmost being; you knit me together in my mother's womb. I praise you because I am fearfully and wonderfully made; your works are wonderful, I know that full well. My frame was not hidden from you when I was made in the secret place. When I was woven together in the depths of the earth, your eyes saw my unformed body. All the days ordained for me were written in your book before one of them came to be. *(Psalm 139:13-16)* You are the salt of the earth. But if the salt loses its saltiness, how can it be made salty again? It is no longer good for anything, except to be thrown out and trampled by men. You are the light of the world. A city on a hill cannot be hidden. *(Matthew 5:13-14)* Yet to all who received him, to those who believed in his name, he gave the right to become children of God—children born not of natural descent, nor of human decision or a husband's will, but born of God. *(John 1:12-13)* I no longer call you servants, because a servant does not know his master's business. Instead, I have called you friends, for everything that I learned from my Father I have made known to you. *(John 15:15)* Therefore, if anyone is in Christ, he is a new creation; the old has gone, the new has come! All this is from God, who reconciled us to himself through Christ and gave us the ministry of reconciliation: that God was reconciling the world to himself in Christ, not counting men's sins against them. And he has committed to us the message of reconciliation. We are therefore Christ's ambassadors, as though God were making his appeal through us. We implore you on Christ's behalf: Be reconciled to God. God made him who had no sin to be sin for us, so that in him we might become the righteousness of God. *(2 Corinthians 5:17-21)* Because you are sons, God sent the Spirit of his Son into our hearts, the Spirit who calls out, "Abba, Father." So you are no longer a slave, but a son; and since you are a son, God has made you also an heir. *(Galatians 4:6-7)* For we are God's workmanship, created in Christ Jesus to do good works, which God prepared in advance for us to do. *(Ephesians 2:10)* Therefore, as God's chosen people, holy and dearly loved, clothe yourselves with compassion, kindness, humility, gentleness and patience. *(Colossians 3:12)*

> **God's story answers the big questions** in our lives. It tells us *who God says we are,* helping each of us to understand our own identity. This is a powerful part of your story that others need to hear.

3.2 Notes

From what you saw last week in God's story, which attributes of God's character (what he is like) are most comforting and relevant to you and your story so far?

Do you find it easy or difficult to pray to God as "Abba Father" (Daddy)? Why or why not?

How often during a normal day do you connect your story, experiences and life-perspectives to the truth found in God's story (the Bible)?

How does the truth that God has been writing you into his story since before creation affect you?

3.3

There are four distinct movements within God's story found in the Bible: *creation, fall, redemption,* and *restoration.*

Every person has these same four parts in their story, and today you will begin to look at your story in light of this pattern. Ask the Holy Spirit to show you which parts you should include as you begin to craft your gospel story. Let this process shape and change how you see your own life and what God is doing in and through you today.

Following are some questions to think about. Use these as guidelines to help you create parts of your story in the Notes section on the following two pages.

Creation

How did your life begin? Describe your family and others and the moments that shaped you as a person before you began to be a disciple of Jesus?

Share something really great or really hard that happened early in your life. This might be the influence of good or bad friends, music and films, or other experiences that shaped you in significant ways.

Key Question: *Who or what most shaped your understanding of yourself? What were the sources of your sense of personal value and identity?*

Fall

What was happening in your life that was *broken?* In other words, in what ways was it NOT the way God created you to be? Relationships? Health? Addictions? Bad choices? What types of sin were you falling into and what were the effects?

This may feel difficult or risky for you, but be sure to include specific sins from your life (behaviors *and* attitudes). What types of things did you try to use to "fix" your life?

As you identify your own personal history of sin, work to understand it in light of the story of God. Remember, all of our choices that contradict his story and his ways are sin.

Key Question: *How was your relationship with God and others NOT the way God created it to be? Why?*

Redemption

Explain how the effects of sin in your life were rescued and redeemed by Jesus's life, death and resurrection. The good news of Jesus is always personal, expressed in the ways our lives have been changed by Christ. Be sure to include how you came to find out about and begin to walk with Jesus. Was there a special person or community that helped you along the way?

Key Question: *How did you come to put your trust in him to save you and restore your life to the way God intended it to be? How has your life been rescued by Jesus's sacrifice?*

Restoration

What is happening in your life now? How is God changing you, using you, speaking to you now that he has redeemed you from the penalty of your sins and is restoring you from the effects of past sins.

Be sure to include at least two examples of how the gospel (Jesus at work in your life) is changing and re-creating your life, relationships (with God and others) or any other part of your life that is being restored. This is where the good news of the gospel and what Jesus has done shows up in your everyday life.

Key Question: *What has changed and what is changing in your life now? Who and what is the focus of your life today?*

3.3 Notes

Think about these movements in your life and write down some of the major pieces of your story here. Tomorrow you will pull it all together into a 3-5 minute story. Plan on spending a little more time on this tomorrow than usual. Try and set aside at least 90 minutes of uninterrupted time.

CREATION

The key question is: Who or what most shaped who you thought you were, and where you got your real value and "identity" in life from?

FALL

The key question here is: Why was your relationship with God and others, (and anything else in your life), NOT the way it was supposed to be? (as God created it...)

REDEMPTION

The key question is: How has Jesus paid the penalty for your sins (when he died on the cross), and how did you come to put your faith and trust in him to save and restore your life to the way God intended it to be?

RESTORATION

The key question is: What has changed and is changing in your life now? AND who and what is the focus of your life today?

3.4

ACTION

Writing Your Gospel Story

Today you'll be pulling together all the pieces from the "4 Key Questions" work you did yesterday. Write this as a narrative either on paper or on a computer so you can capture everything and practice telling it. Ask the Spirit to guide you.

Remember, your story is a part of the ultimate story—God's story. Even though you are telling your personal story here, the end result should focus on God and how Jesus rescued and saved you. Remember God is the hero of your story!

TIPS FOR WRITING YOUR STORY

* MAKE YOUR STORY ABOUT 3-5 MINUTES LONG (A LITTLE OVER 1000 WORDS).

* DON'T GET PREACHY OR CHURCHY. JUST TELL YOUR REAL STORY.

* USE NORMAL, EVERYDAY LANGUAGE.

* KEEP GOD AND JESUS THE MAIN CHARACTERS IN YOUR STORY. DON'T IGNORE THE ROUGH PARTS, BUT DON'T FOCUS ON HOW BAD YOU WERE EI- THER. JUST MAKE JESUS LOOK AWESOME!

* DON'T WORRY ABOUT WHAT OTHERS WILL THINK OF YOUR STORY. REMEMBER IT'S YOUR STORY, THEY CAN'T REALLY ARGUE WITH WHAT HAS HAP- PENED IN YOUR LIFE.

* DON'T TRY AND TELL EVERY SINGLE TRUTH ABOUT GOD OR THE BIBLE IN YOUR STORY. LET PEOPLE ASK QUESTIONS AS YOU GO OR AT THE END AND THEN FILL IN THE DETAILS.

NOTE: THERE ARE 2 SAMPLE STORIES IN THE APPENDIX TO GIVE YOU SOME EXAMPLES.

TIPS FOR WHEN AND WHERE TO TELL YOUR STORY IN THE FUTURE:

* WHEN YOUR RELATIONSHIP WITH SOMEONE GOES BEYOND SUPERFICIAL.

* WHEN FRIENDS START TO ASK YOU QUESTIONS ABOUT YOUR LIFE AND PAST.

* WHEN SOMEONE ASKS YOU A "SPIRITUAL" OR "RELIGIOUS" QUESTION.

* WHEN JESUS, CHURCH OR RELIGION COMES UP IN CONVERSATION.

* WHEN A FRIEND IS HAVING HARD TIMES OR SERIOUS LIFE PROBLEMS.

* WHEN SOMEONE IS CURIOUS ABOUT WHY YOU ARE DIFFERENT OR SEEM TO BE AT PEACE.

* WHEN YOU FEEL LIKE YOU ARE GETTING MORE SERIOUS IN A ROMANTIC RELATIONSHIP AND YOU WANT TO UNDERSTAND WHERE THE OTHER PERSON IS AT IN THEIR BELIEFS.

* WHEN GOD IS PROMPTING YOU TO SHARE YOUR FAITH WITH SOMEONE.

...YOUR STORY IS A PERFECT WAY TO RESPOND!

3.5
COMMUNITY

Sharing Your Gospel Story

Make sure you have enough time today to give each
person in your group 3-5 minutes to tell their story
and a little time to answer questions.

Today, take time to practice telling your gospel stories
to each other. Sit in a circle, not at a table, but in a living room or comfortable setting. Be sure to set up an
environment that is quiet enough to hear well. Make
this time as normal and relaxed as possible. Give each
person 3-5 minutes to tell their story.

Listen carefully and be prepared to ask questions.
Pray prayers of thanksgiving for each person after they
have finished reading (or telling) their story.

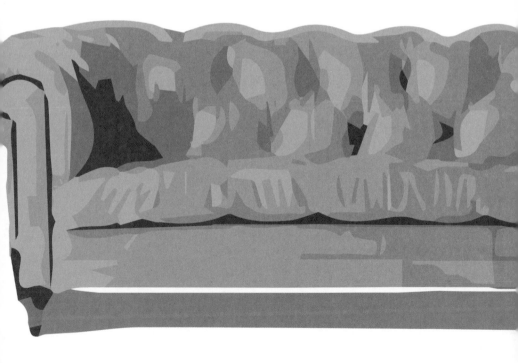

A word about words...

It seems that many of us are bilingual. We speak in one normal, everyday language most of the time, but when it comes time to talk about religion, spirituality, God, Jesus or church we break out our special "Christianese" language.

I have often heard Christians use words and phrases like *sanctified, filled with the Spirit, washed in Jesus' blood, glorified, Jesus in your heart* and a whole host of other terms gleaned from years of singing praise and worship music. Some of it comes from hearing other Christians talk this way. Some from the fact that most sermons we've heard use A LOT of this special language.

But if we want to tell our stories in ways that others who have not learned this unusual dialect will relate to and connect with, we need to retrain ourselves to proclaim the gospel using language that communicates good news in words that the listener will understand.

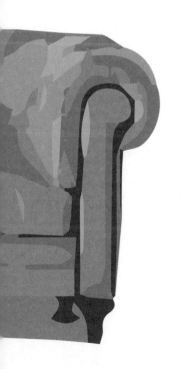

Questions:

When you listened to each other tell your story today, did you hear any words that you didn't really understand or that would not really come up in normal, everyday conversation? What were they? How else might we explain what we mean without talking in "code"?

How were your grandparents raised? Where did they live? How many children did they have? **How did your parents meet?** Did they come to faith in Jesus? How? Think of all the friends and acquaintances you've had throughout life. How have they changed you? **Where in your life has there been pain or loss? How about joy and great victory?** What are the experiences that have shaped you? **What books, movies, and songs have made you see life differently?** Have there been specific conversations that nudged you toward the truth and love of Christ? **What else?**

"Let us fix our eyes on Jesus, the author and perfecter of our faith." [Hebrews 12:2]

It's easy to think that the only point where our story intersected with God's story was when we made a "decision" or said a special prayer at our conversion experience. And while that is definitely a major crossroads for us and an important part of our story, the truth is that God has been connected to our story long before our birth and before we ever came to know and trust him. If we look closely, we see that throughout our history are points where God intersected our story for his glory (sorry about the rhyme...but it's true!)

Where in your life are you still longing for more—more intimacy, more healing and growth, more forgiveness, significance or recognition? These are all places that God is waiting to intersect your story with the power of the gospel. Remember, the gospel didn't happen—it is still happening in your life. God is still writing new chapters in your story and he is the perfect author of life.

3.6 Notes

How has your perspective on the future changed after writing and sharing your gospel story?

Are there parts of your story that you are still afraid or ashamed to share? Tell them to God now in prayer. Remember...these things have ALL been redeemed and are now being re-created by the gospel!

What parts of your story from the past are still needing to be re-created and restored?

What parts of your life today are still being redeemed?

Where in your life are you putting your hope in a different "hero" to come and save and restore you (self, spouse, boss, money, talents, etc.)? Confess this to God as sin and ask him to be your rescuer.

In what ways do you think your relationships will change with the others in your group after both sharing your story and hearing theirs?

"For I know the plans I have for you," declares the LORD, "plans to prosper you and not to harm you, plans to give you hope and a future." [Jeremiah 29:11]

Praise be to the God and Father of our Lord Jesus Christ, who has blessed us in the heavenly realms with every spiritual blessing in Christ. For he chose us in him before the creation of the world to be holy and blameless in his sight. In love he predestined us for adoption to sonship through Jesus Christ, in accordance with his pleasure and will to the praise of his glorious grace, which he has freely given us in the One he loves. [Ephesians 1:3-6]

Consider This:

You and your story were a part of God's plan before time began. And God has always planned to bless you immensely through his son, Jesus. Take time today to prayerfully give all of your future plans, hopes and dreams to him. The pressure is off—you can rest in a hope and future that is secure in his perfect love and strength!

WEEK 4

Gospel Listening

Listening is a magnetic and strange thing, a creative force. The friends who listen to us are the ones we move toward. When we are listened to, it creates us, makes us unfold and expand.   - Karl Menninger

Listening for the Story

I was walking through a Barnes and Noble bookstore the other day and I saw a lady reading a book to about thirty children who had their eyes and their total attention locked on the details of every sentence she read.

Stories can be transformational, both God's and our own, when they get inside us and affect the way we live. Our own personal stories follow the patterns and themes found in the story of God.

In fact, when we start to look closely, the story of God is embedded in everyone's personal story. Even the smaller stories that make up our everyday lives—stuff from work, parenting, a trip to the mall, or vacation stories—when we examine them, we often discover that they too follow the pattern of Creation ➡ Fall ➡ Redemption ➡ Restoration.

All of these stories—the big life stories and the smaller stories that make up our daily lives and relationships—offer an immediate and powerful way to listen for opportunities to speak good news into a person's life and circumstance. The gospel addresses all of life, and when we practice gospel listening we can grow in our ability to address others' circumstances from a gospel perspective.

Let the wise listen and add to their learning, and let the discerning get guidance. [Proverbs 1:5]

4.1 Notes

Why do you think that most of us are such poor listeners?

What or who are we often focused on when others are talking?
Why is this?

What types of things need to change in your heart and posture in order to make you a better listener?

How does it make you feel when someone really listens to you?

Who in your life has modeled good listening skills? What can you learn from them?

4.2

MEDITATION

Throughout God's story we find that he is a very good listener. He often asked questions that he obviously knew the answers to, just to reveal a person's heart and draw them closer in relationship. In this way, God shows his love, patience, presence and care for us too.

Spend some time today reading the stories surrounding these verses. Notice God's/Jesus' posture when dealing with people and how it reveals his heart and theirs.

"Where are you?"
(Genesis 3)
God pursues Adam after he has sinned.

"Who has made man's mouth?"
(Exodus 4)
God addresses Moses' fear to speak on God's behalf.

"Where were you when I laid the earth's foundation?"
(Job 38)
God reminds Job about the limits of his knowledge and God's greatness.

"Who is like Me?"
(Isaiah 44)
God declares his greatness to Israel.

"Who do you say that I am?"
(Mark 8)
Jesus seeks his disciples thoughts about his true identity.

"Who is my mother, and who are my brothers?"
(Matthew 12)
Jesus clarifies who his true family is.

"What do you want me to do for you?"
(Matthew 20)
Jesus responds to a man in need.

4.2 Notes

God is an amazing servant-listener.... How about you? Do you consider yourself a good listener? Would others consider you a good listener?

On a scale of 1 to 10 where would you rate yourself on the "good listener" scale?

With your friends?

1-----2-----3-----4-----5-----6-----7-----8-----9-----10

With "teachers" in your life?

1-----2-----3-----4-----5-----6-----7-----8-----9-----10

With your parents?

1-----2-----3-----4-----5-----6-----7-----8-----9-----10

With God?

1-----2-----3-----4-----5-----6-----7-----8-----9-----10

What questions might God be asking you right now in your life?

4.3

CHANGE

Even before beginning to follow Jesus and understanding life from the perspective of God's story, every person has these same four parts to their story—and in all the countless little stories and narratives that flow out in normal conversation. Let's take a look at each part again from the perspective of gospel listening.

creation

Everyone has a fundamental belief about their origin—who or what gave them their existence, made them who they are, or shaped them into the person they are today.

Listen for: *Who or what do they credit or blame for who they are today? Or the situation they find themselves in?*

fall

Each person has a central belief about the cause of brokenness in the world and a deep desire for justice. People blame their parents, family, friends, boss, government, etc. for what they've become AND want justice by putting the blame on someone else for the pain and suffering in the (their) world. Someone is at fault and someone deserves punishment.

Listen for: *Why are things and people not the way they are supposed to be and who is to blame?*

redemption

Everyone has a solution they believe in, a remedy they look to or a "savior" they trust in to redeem the brokenness in their life and world. Many are looking to a philosophy. Others look to a plan for self-improvement or personal growth. Many believe some kind of reform in education or politics will change things. Everyone believes in a "redeemer" or in a self-Improvement plan of some sort.

Listen for: *Who or what will rescue them and redeem what is broken in their life?*

restoration

Every person has a picture of the future when everything is as it should be...or how they hope it will be. Some see a utopia with humans all living at peace with one another. Others believe Mother Earth and humanity will be one. Still others see another world they will go to where they will be at the center. Some people's future hope is to be married, have children, get a job, be rich, etc. Everyone wants something better—restoration of what they believe their world should be like.

Listen for: *What will the world or their circumstance look like when all is as it should be (according to them), AND who or what will be the focus of this world?*

4.3 Notes

When you think about all the conversations you have in any given day, week or month, how does this perspective of gospel listening affect the level of importance you place on each conversation?

How should this reality that God is in all the little details of everyone's story change the way that you listen?

Why do you think that being a good listener is a display of what God is really like?

What does it communicate to others when we take the time to focus in, ask good questions and truly listen to them?

NOTE: Read through tomorrow's Action in the primer so that you will be prepared. You will need to think through "who and when" to fully engage tomorrow's action...not waiting until later in the day to read or work through things.

ACTION

CREATION
→FALL
→REDEMPTION
→RESTORATION

Think of at least three people from among your friends, spouse, children, siblings, fellow-students, co-workers or neighbors that you can practice gospel listening with.

Engage these three people today in separate conversations. Nothing big or crazy, just normal, everyday discussions. Ask a few questions about their day or life recently and LISTEN! You do not have to try and "fix" this person or evangelize them. Today, just practice listening to what they say through the lens of creation, fall, redemption, and restoration.

Listen to where or how their stories begin, or how things used to be.

Listen for what is now broken and not the way they used to be or how the person wants it.

Listen for what they think will ultimately "fix" their situation.

Listen for what they are ultimately thinking life or this situation will be like when all is well.

Learn to listen to whatever a person is complaining about or super excited about when they talk. What they are complaining about usually fits into the "Fall" part of that particular story. This gives you a good idea of where they need the good news in place of their "bad news."

What they're excited about may be part of the "Redemption" or "Restoration" piece of their story. Is the person or thing they are putting their hope in (for redemption) going to ultimately last and satisfy them? Are their hopes for the future in line with God's plans for them in light of the gospel?

4.5
COMMUNITY

Here are three sample "mini-stories" that could come up in normal conversation. As a group, identify the movements (creation, fall, redemption, restoration) and discuss what the good news would be for this person. (You may want to review some of what we learned in sections 1.2 and 1.4.)

STORY I

"When I first started working here I had the best boss in the world. He was so appreciative of my work and performance. Then he got transferred to another department and my new supervisor is a complete fool! He doesn't know what he is doing and is never happy with me or my work. I'll never get that raise I was hoping for this year. I wish my old boss would come back so I could make some real money!"

Hints: Who/what is this person's ultimate provision? Is their true identity and worth found in the eyes of their boss? Will money or more possessions bring lasting happiness and joy? Would praying for them to get their old boss back lead them toward trusting in God more or less?

STORY 2

"We started out as best friends. When Nick and I first got married we did everything together and spent SO much time just talking. I know it sounds corny, but he really completed me. Now his stupid job keeps him at work 50-60 hours a week. The baby wears me out completely and we both just flop down exhausted in front of the TV after she's tucked into bed. We rarely have deep, meaningful conversations and I hardly know who I am anymore. Does Nick still love me? Maybe I just need to work harder on our marriage so things will be like they were before."

Hints: Which relationship in her life is she looking to for ultimate fulfillment? Is there One who will perfectly meet her emotional/ spiritual needs forever? Where is she placing her hope for their mar- riage and future?

STORY 3

"My teacher is always telling us how smart and artistic Amy is and that the rest of our class could learn a thing or two from her. No matter how hard I try I can never get the grades she did. Well yesterday, it turns out she was caught cheating. I have to admit it was pretty awesome to see her knocked down a peg. Ahhh, sweet justice! Wait 'til I see her again...Now maybe the rest of us will get a little more attention from Mr. Phipps."

Hints: Is our performance what makes us loved and accepted? What level of grace have we received in light of our own offenses in life? What is true justice in light of the gospel that restores all things?

And one more thing...

Have someone in your group tell about the most frustrating part of their week, or something that is currently a problem for them. Ask them a few questions and try and see where the pattern of Creation ➜ Fall ➜ Redemption ➜ Restoration comes up. It may not seem to fit perfectly, but it's there and will give you perspectives to listen from.

Go deep: *Speak the truth of the gospel—what is now true for them because of Jesus' life, death and resurrection—into their situation. Be gentle and caring. Listen to their responses to see if what you are saying is good news to them.*

Partnership with the Holy Spirit

Gospel listening is real-time partnering with the Holy Spirit, asking him to give you wisdom and insight into what is really going on in a person's heart. Sometimes we can only guess at what is really going on under the surface, but the Spirit knows the hearts of everyone perfectly.

Learning to allow the Holy Spirit to reveal the hidden sin or the unbelief behind the attitude is a big part of growing in gospel listening and our overall gospel fluency.

As you listen to someone's story (or consider your own), notice the reasons for not being willing or able to obey Jesus's commands: fear, insecurities, selfishness, pride, need for approval, and the worship of children, family or work. All of these reflect trust placed in something or someone other than God.

As you become aware of the people or things that have become idols or "little gods," take the time to compare them to Jesus. Ask the Holy Spirit to help in revealing Jesus as the best resolution to what a person is seeking elsewhere, the opposite of what they are experiencing, and the deeper reality of what they are searching for.

Here are some sample questions that can be used to get at the heart motives behind a person's words and actions (or our own.)

Why is this so important to you?

Why is this upsetting you?

How would God's view of you change if this did/didn't change or work out?

Who is ultimately responsible for this in your world?

Hows that working for you?

Are you finding deep satisfaction from this thing or person?

What if that goes away?

4.6 Notes

Using the questions on the previous page, practice "gospel listening" to your own heart through the answers you give concerning the following issues:

1. The most frustrating person, thing or situation in your life right now.
2. What is giving you the greatest hope for the future right now?
3. What things in your life do you think God is pleased about right now?
4. Is your concern for money or desires for things making it hard to enjoy God and simple living?
5) What are your hopes and dreams for your spouse and kids or close friends?

Write down your thoughts.

4.7

ReCREATE

You have searched me, Lord, and you know me.
You know when I sit and when I rise; you perceive my
thoughts from afar.

Where can I go from your Spirit?
Where can I flee from your presence?

Search me, God, and know my heart; test me and know my
anxious thoughts.

See if there is any offensive way in me, and lead me in the
way everlasting.

from Psalm 139

Consider This:
The best news about the gospel is that we can come clean and speak to God like we would speak to our most trusted friend.

Have you been 100% honest with him? Tell him what you are concerned about, ticked off about, confused about and hopeful about. He can take it!

Four Eternal Truths

5.1

EXPLORATION

I cannot believe I did that again!

Where does sin come from? Why do we still sin even after we have acknowledged something as sin, and perhaps, repented of it over and over?

My friend Tim Chester once said, "Sinful acts always have their origin in some form of unbelief; behind every sin is a lie. The root of all our behavior and emotions is the heart, what it trusts and what it treasures. People are given over to sinful desires because 'they exchanged the truth about God for a lie'" (Romans 1:25).[2] This forever changed my view of sin.

"Everything that does not come from faith is sin" (Romans 14:23).

Another word for faith is "belief," and these verses suggest that all sin comes from not believing what is true about God. Typically people want to blame their sin on their circumstances—I got angry because the guy cut me off in traffic, I started to worry all the time because my husband lost his job, I yelled at the kids because they weren't obeying me....

But the reality is our circumstances merely illuminate what is already in our hearts. Our struggles reveal our hearts.

This heart-level perspective is a radical view of sin and repentance. But this perspective is also a helpful view of sin and transformation, because it very clearly shows us the way out of our struggle. Most of us think that the way to stop sinning is to change our behavior. But, if behind every sin is a lie about God, then **what really needs to change is what I am believing in my heart.**

The four eternal truths about God, when not fully believed, lead to every area of sin in our lives. If you are anything like me, when I first heard these "4 G's" I was immediately convicted by the Spirit that I had unbelief in one or two of these areas.

Stress, fears, performance issues, ungratefulness, and **striving**: notice that all of these are heart issues. There is always a heart issue behind every sinful action.

How about you?

There is much more that could be said about God than is covered by these four truths, but they give us a powerful diagnostic tool for addressing most of the sins and negative emotions that cause us to struggle. As we walk through the rest of this week we'll unpack each of these truths and the potential lies we believe about God in greater detail. For now, let this simmer, giving the Holy Spirit room to shine some light into your heart.

The 4 G's

Four eternal truths about God:

God is Great...
so I don't have to be in control.

God is Glorious...
so I don't have to fear others.

God is Good...
so I don't have to look elsewhere for
my satisfaction.

God is Gracious...
so I don't have to prove myself.

5.1 Notes

When you think of "sin" do you usually think of actions (do's and don'ts) or attitudes and beliefs? Why?

What would change if you started to look for "the unbelief behind the sin" in your life and in the lives of others?

Which of the 4 G's immediately grabbed your attention? Why?

When do you most struggle with sin? What ultimately triggers sin in your life?

What failed "sin management" techniques have you employed in the past?

5.2
MEDITATION

IF YOU CONFESS WITH YOUR MOUTH, "JESUS IS LORD," AND BELIEVE IN YOUR HEART THAT GOD RAISED HIM FROM THE DEAD, YOU WILL BE SAVED. FOR IT IS WITH YOUR HEART THAT YOU BELIEVE AND ARE JUSTIFIED, AND IT IS WITH YOUR MOUTH THAT YOU CONFESS AND ARE SAVED.

(ROMANS 10:9-10)

What does it mean to believe?

According to the Bible, our hearts are far more than just a muscle in our chests pumping blood throughout our bodies.

In fact, the word *heart* occurs over 850 times in the Bible.

Our *heart* makes decisions, feels emotion, can be deceived, desires things, lusts, thinks, and reasons. The word *heart* is the word the Bible uses to describe the real you, the very center of your being. The heart includes your mind, emotions and will. It is not less than any one of those things; it is more.

The truth is we *believe* with our hearts. Think about it. Do you believe with your head? No. Ultimately, you believe in your heart, the deepest part of who you are: your mind, your emotions and your will.

5.2 Notes

Unbelievers... All of us!

Not many Christians think of themselves as unbelievers. We normally use the term to describe people who are sojourners and not yet disciples of Jesus. But there are many things about God that we actually do not believe. Often there is a large gap between what we say we believe in our head, and what we truly believe in our heart.

I call this our *Head/Heart Distortion.*

The process of closing the gap between what we know in our head and what we believe in our heart is called *sanctification.* Sanctification is about becoming more like Jesus, but we will only become more like Jesus when our actions are consistent with what we say we believe.

Where in your experience have you believed one thing in your head, but acted out of a different heart motive, belief or perception? (There are probably several. Try and write down at least 3 or 4.)

Write down areas of your life that...
...cause you to be stressed.

...make you crave approval.

...you often complain about.

...you are overly sensitive about.

5.3

CHANGE

The Truth Shall Set You Free

Let's take a deeper look at the lies we believe, some of the evidence that this is true, and how the truth about God can set us free from sin in each of these areas.

God is Great...
so I don't have to be in control.

We may know (and even say we believe) that God is in control of all things—that he is sovereign—but then we are filled with worry and anxiety about many of the details of our lives. It's as if we're saying, "I know in my head that God is in control, but I don't

God is Glorious...
so I don't have to fear others.

One common reason we sin is that we crave the approval of others or fear their rejection or disapproval. We "need" the acceptance of a parent, boss, friend, spouse, etc., so we are controlled by them and their opinion of us. The Bible's term for this is "fear of man."

"Fear of man will prove to be a snare, but whoever trusts in the Lord is kept safe."
(Proverbs 29:25)

Great Glorious

really believe in my heart that God is in control...or maybe he needs my help. Therefore, I must work to control certain people or situations in my life." Ouch.

But if I truly believe that God is great, that he is large and in charge of EVERYTHING in life, then I can rest and repent of stressing out over people, circumstances or my future.

The answer to fear of man is fear of God. We need a bigger, better, more glorious view of God. The word glory means "weighty," as in "a person of importance, a weighty person." God should be the "weightiest" person in our lives.

Imagine Jesus standing next to the person you most fear or seek approval from in your life. Who is more glorious? Remember, the most glorious One in the universe loves you, laid his life down to have you in a relationship with him, and is crazy about you!

God is Good...
so I don't have to look elsewhere for my satisfaction.

God created humanity to be needy. He gave us continual reminders of our need for him and his ongoing provision: hunger, thirst, exhaustion, need for love, relationship, and intimacy. None of these can be fulfilled from within ourselves. We were designed to need God.

When we look for fulfillment and satisfaction for these needs elsewhere in life, we

Jesus came to satisfy the hunger of our souls, to give us rest, to live in an intimate and loving relationship with us. Jesus is the better fulfilment for our every need.

God is Gracious...
so I don't have to prove myself (to my self, to others, to God).

We can spend our life trying to prove ourselves worthy, valuable or right. I want to prove to myself that I am good enough or desirable. We strive to impress others and constantly seek their validation and approval. Ultimately, we try to impress God with our lives so that he will bless us or be happy with us.

The grace of God is so simple to understand

become bitter and complaining because people and things eventually fail to deeply satisfy our souls and the needs God created in us.

Instead of seeking ultimate satisfaction from food, drink, exercise, sleep, sex, or relationships, we need to trust the only One who can truly satisfy our needy hearts.

and yet so hard to grasp. We seem to be hard-wired to think we must do something to make God look and act favorably toward us. But while we were still sinners, he sent his son Jesus to die in our place—the ultimate act of his grace toward us. When we really believe in our hearts that God is gracious we will stop trying to prove ourselves and earn his love.

5.3 Notes

Control is the other side of the coin of stress or fear. When do you most feel the need to control things? Or people?

What fears do you have concerning the future? How does the truth that God is great change how you feel?

When it comes to your self-worth, whose affirmation do you seek the most?

What parts of your life are you most worried about what others think?

In *The Weight of Glory*, C.S. Lewis states: "We are half-hearted creatures, fooling about with drink and sex and ambition when infinite joy is offered us, like an ignorant child who wants to go on making mud pies in a slum because he cannot imagine what is meant by the offer of a holiday at the sea. We are far too easily pleased."

When or how have you sought satisfaction that was ultimately a pale comparison to the "better" that God has offered? (relationships, food, alcohol, achievement, entertainment, etc.)

Where in your life are you saying, "I know God is good, but..."? What do you most complain about?

What "spiritual" things are you doing, secretly thinking you are impressing God? (Bible reading, church attendance, tithing, serving)

How long does it take you to forgive yourself when you sin or perform badly in some part of your life?

5.4

ACTION

Spend some time in prayer working through the 4 G's. Ask the Holy Spirit to reveal potential areas of sin and unbelief in your life. Think especially about those stubborn areas of sin that never seem to change; we all have them. Think about areas of fear and frustration in your life. Remember, every sin comes from believing a lie about God that can be replaced by an accurate belief in what is true about him. You may want to review or use the questions from yesterday to help guide this time. Write down your thoughts using the categories below.

Area of Sin, Frustration, or Fear	Lie about God	Truth about God

Don't skip this part: Now take some time with a close friend or spouse and ask them to go through each of the 4 G's with you and give their input on what the Spirit revealed to you. Ask them to confirm if they have seen this in your life and invite them to offer any additions to your list.

GOD IS GREAT...SO I DON'T HAVE TO BE IN CONTROL. GOD IS GLORIOUS... SO I DON'T HAVE TO FEAR OTHERS. GOD IS GOOD...SO I DON'T HAVE TO LOOK ELSEWHERE FOR MY SATIS-FACTION. GOD IS GRACIOUS...SO I DON'T HAVE TO PROVE MYSELF.

We've found it helpful to have a copy of the 4G's posted around the house (maybe on the refrigerator or the bathroom mirror.) Or you can print a small copy of it and keep it in a wallet or purse. You may want to photocopy this page (or page 99) and put it somewhere that will help you to remember these four eternal truths throughout your day.

To say to temptation *"I must not do this"* is legalism. To say *"I need not do this because God is bigger and better"* is good news.

- Tim Chester

Today as a community we want to go a little deeper with each other. We want to practice "gospeling" ourselves and others. *So let's dive in!*

Go around the group and have each person take turns sharing a current area of frustration or fear that they are facing from the lists you created yesterday. Take about 10 minutes per person, more if needed.

Discuss these as a group, gently helping the person move from unbelief to belief by reminding them what is true about God (one of the 4 G's) and how this truth is best displayed in the life, death and resurrection of Jesus. Stop and pray for that person before moving on to the next.

Read these two examples and then try it with your group...

Fear
"I am afraid that my father won't approve of my changing career tracks and I don't want him to be disappointed in me."

Truth Response
"God is the most glorious one in the universe and he loves and approves of you because of what Jesus did on the cross. You have his love regardless of what you choose concerning your career."

Frustration
"I am really tired of arguing with my co-workers over things that I know we should do differently!"

Truth Response
"God is great and you don't have to control others, in fact you can't control whether they agree with you or not. Rest in the knowledge that God alone can truly change hearts and attitudes. God proved his great love for you and them when he sent Jesus to rescue and restore us all."

5.6

CALIBRATION

Identifying our idols

Growing up in the church, whenever I heard the word idol or idolatry I thought of little stone statues or totem poles.

No problem with those in my life...check!

But idols are anything or anyone in our life that we put above God, in any way. Our hearts are like idol factories; we hardly go a moment without placing our hope or trust in something or someone other than Jesus to fulfill us or make us whole. Or we "serve" idols that give us the feelings or status we long for.

But we can learn to identify the idols of the heart that seek to control us, and speak gospel truth into those dark and destructive beliefs and desires.

Ultimately, Jesus is the great, glorious, good and gracious one who crushes the idols of our heart. Now that we are starting to see how these truths apply to our lives, let's take it a little further and uncover the way idols lurk and hide behind the corners of our life.

Take a look at these four idols that grow into many others.[3] Then notice which of the 4 G's sets us free from the idol and how Jesus is our ultimate fulfillment and satisfaction.

CONTROL

Desire:
Self-discipline, certainty, strict standards

Price We Will Pay:
Overworked, loneliness

Greatest Nightmare:
Uncertainty

Others Often Feel:
Condemned, pushed

Problem Emotion:
Worry, fear

Eternal Truth:
God is great, so I don't have to be in control (of people or situations). Jesus was raised from the dead when it seemed that all was lost.

COMFORT

Desire:
Privacy, lack of stress, freedom, easy life

Price We Will Pay:
Ineffectiveness, selfishness

Greatest Nightmare:
Stress, demands, pain or loss

Others Often Feel:
Hurt

Problem Emotion:
Boredom, discontentment

Eternal Truth:
God is good, so I don't have to look elsewhere for my satisfaction. Jesus is the Father's greatest gift to us and he is enough.

APPROVAL

Desire:
Affirmation, love, relationship

Price We Will Pay:
Inauthenticity, codependency

Greatest Nightmare:
Rejection

Others Often Feel:
Smothered

Problem Emotion:
Insecurity

Eternal Truth:
God is glorious, so I don't have to fear others. Jesus took our rejection and earned us full approval before the Father.

POWER

Desire:
Success, influence

Price We Will Pay:
Burdened, responsibility

Greatest Nightmare:
Humiliation, lack of respect

Others Often Feel:
Used

Problem Emotion:
Anger

Eternal Truth:
God is gracious, so I don't have to prove myself (to my self, to others, to God). Jesus gave up his authority and power on the cross to secure our position in the kingdom.

5.6 Notes

Turning a good thing in our life into an ultimate thing makes it an idol. What possessions, relationships or situations in your life have moved from healthy to idolatrous? (You can tell by imagining that person or thing gone from your life forever. Could you live without it or them?)

In what ways has control been an idol in your life?

How can the belief that God is greater begin to remove that idol?

In what ways has approval been an idol in your life?

How can the belief that God is more glorious begin to remove that idol?

In what ways has comfort been an idol in your life?

How can the belief that God is always good begin to remove that idol?

In what ways has power been an idol in your life?

How can the belief that God is gracious begin to remove that idol?

Remember...

Faith = Trusting in God instead of believing lies

Repentance = Living in line with what is true about God

5.7

ReCREATE

Jesus declared, *"He who has seen Me has seen the Father."*
[John 14:9]

The Apostle Paul writes, *"He is the image of the invisible God."*
[Colossians 1:15]

The writer of Hebrews proclaimed, *"The Son is the radiance of God's glory and the exact imprint of his nature, sustaining all things by his powerful word."*
[Hebrews 1:3]

Consider This

Jesus is the ultimate demonstration of what God is like. In his life, death and resurrection we see God's greatness, glory, goodness and grace most wonderfully and eternally put on display.

Part of the good news is that Jesus is alive(!) and now sits on the throne interceding on our behalf. We can rest in a life-altering belief that the ongoing work of the gospel in our life is provided and sustained by Jesus himself.

WEEK 6
Two Lenses

6.1

EXPLORATION

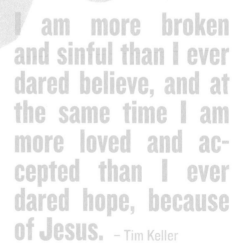

Two Gospel Lenses

Back in the 1950s when 3-D movies were first introduced, the visual effects were not that stunning. They were more novel than awe-inspiring. In recent years, we have seen a big improvement in 3-D technology, but without wearing those nerdy glasses and viewing the film through both special lenses simultaneously, the picture is distorted and not what the director had in mind.

The gospel is like that in some ways too. We can read the Bible thematically, and we can read it as a story. But both "lenses" are necessary, and it takes these two perspectives to fully understand and engage the gospel in its richest form.

I am more broken and sinful than I ever dared believe, and at the same time I am more loved and accepted than I ever dared hope, because of Jesus. – Tim Keller

LENS #1: The Power of the Gospel
Viewed thematically

God: eternal, all powerful Creator
Sin: self-rule chosen over obedience to God; the penalty for sin is separation from God and death
Jesus: God incarnate came to die as a substitute for the penalty of sin
Faith: we are saved by faith in what Jesus did and not by any accomplishment of our own

Here we see the good news that God is completely aware of our sin problem, and in and through the work of Jesus Christ, accepts us and recreates us by the power of his Spirit.

LENS #2: The Purpose of the Gospel
Viewed as a story

Creation ➡ *Fall* ➡ *Redemption* ➡ *Restoration*

Here we see the good news that God sent his Son to redeem the world from the effects of sin and restore all people, places and things to the way he originally created it.

Rebellion, death, decay, injustice, and suffering will all be removed. When everything is restored, God will be seen by all for who he truly is—he will be glorified. This is the kingdom of God in the fullest sense.

6.1 Notes

Which perspective on the gospel are you most familiar with? How often have you heard the gospel presented from both perspectives?

How does your understanding of the gospel change when you add the second "lens"?

Who or what does the first perspective focus on? Who or what does the second perspective focus on?

If the purpose of the gospel is ultimately to restore and re-create all things, how might God want to use you to accomplish that?

6.2
MEDITATION

"This is what the Lord Almighty, the God of Israel, says to all those I carried into exile from Jerusalem to Babylon: 'Build houses and settle down; plant gardens and eat what they produce. Marry and have sons and daughters; find wives for your sons and give your daughters in marriage, so that they too may have sons and daughters. Increase in number there; do not decrease. Also, seek the peace and prosperity of the city to which I have carried you into exile. Pray to the Lord for it, because if it prospers, you too will prosper.'" [Jeremiah 29:4-7]

God's chosen people, Israel, had forgotten their true identity. They were to be God's representatives of what he is truly like (his glory) in the world—his living agents of mercy, justice and restoration. But they began to give him occasional lip service and temple attendance while living only for themselves. So God allowed Israel to be conquered and taken away into exile and slavery in Babylon. Even in this time of trial and discipline, God intended them to live as a blessing to their enemies.

"When Jesus had called the Twelve together, he gave them power and authority to drive out all demons and to cure diseases, and he sent them out to proclaim the kingdom of God and to heal the sick." [Luke 9:1-2]

"Again Jesus said, 'Peace be with you! As the Father has sent me, I am sending you.'" [John 20:21]

Jesus came as the fulfillment of all that God intended Israel to be and do. He came both proclaiming the good news of the kingdom of God, and healing the sick and restoring sight to the blind. The poor, the broken, the lost—everyone—all need to hear and experience the gospel of the kingdom lived out in their midst. As the church, we are now to live not only as the voice of God, but we are to be his hands and feet of reconciliation as well.

6.2 Notes

What is the most redemptive and restorative thing you have done (or participated in) on behalf of your neighborhood or city?

Have you ever thought that everything God has given you (time, talents, education, resources) have all been entrusted to you for his glory and the work of the gospel?

What percentage of your time do you spend in ways that are restorative in your community?

How might you use your talents and skills as a blessing and display of the gospel to others?

How could you share your education and the experiences God has given you with others for their good?

Do you prioritize your resources, money, and things around self and family first or kingdom and mission first? How could you begin to make changes in this for the sake of the gospel?

What organizations are doing the most to regularly bless the people of your city? (single moms, homeless, at-risk youth, the elderly, the business community, schools, etc.)

In what ways can you, or together as a missional community, partner with and extend the blessing and prosperity those organizations bring?

How could you serve them and be a visual or verbal proclamation of the gospel?

6.3

CHANGE

Gospel Distortion

There is a risk of distorting the gospel when we view it through only one of these two lenses. If we view the gospel primarily as the power that sets us free, we could end up focused on our own personal salvation; getting out of hell and going to heaven some day—a very human-centered gospel.

However, if we view the gospel as purely focused on the restoration of all things, we can tip over the other way and believe and proclaim a social gospel. This is seen in the churches that are centered primarily on doing good works, acts of service and large social projects in their cities, but rarely moving toward a proclamation of the gospel that includes sin, repentance and salvation found in Christ alone.

It is when we grasp and wrestle with both perspectives that we have a gospel that places our salvation squarely on the work of Jesus on the cross and sends us out to be his body, his family of redemption and restoration in the world. It is when the world both hears the good news and sees a demonstration of restoration that they are most inclined to believe. This is a BIG gospel— the gospel of the kingdom that Jesus was talking about!

When we repent of our sin and receive the new life Jesus has offered us, we begin a journey of restoration inside and out. And not just for us—but for the entire world! We are now called to both proclaim the good news and demonstrate it.

God, in Jesus Christ, has given us both the **MESSAGE** of reconciliation and the **MINISTRY** of reconciliation.

[2 Corinthians 5:17-19]

6.3 Notes

Sometimes we swing between "message" and "ministry" depending on the circumstance or environment we are in. What do you most naturally gravitate to: talking about the message of good news and Jesus (proclamation) or serving others as a display of the gospel (demonstration)?

Place an "X" on the line to evaluate, for each situation, where you are most often on this scale.

With co-workers

Proclamation_____Demonstration

With my neighbors

Proclamation_____Demonstration

With others in my family

Proclamation_____Demonstration

With other Christians

Proclamation_____Demonstration

Insight: Don't just think of your non-believing friends in light of this. Look back at the diagram on 1.6. Remember that even as Christians we need the gospel in all of life. So when we think of both proclaiming and demonstrating the gospel, it is just as important that we consistently do this with each other, in Christ.

In the situations where you are farthest to one side of the scale or the other, what would it look like to live out of the full, two lenses of the gospel? How can you bring a better balance to things?

Is there anything keeping you from proclaiming good news in a certain situation, or with certain people?

What is keeping you from a greater demonstration of the gospel?

6.4
ACTION

Grab a pencil and paper and take a walk through your neighborhood. Watch for things you see that remind you of the story and the way God created things. Take note of anything you see that is not in line with God's original plans for people and this world. These are all things that God wants to restore and recreate. If you live somewhat close to any of the others from your group, consider doing this together.

Write down 5 things you saw that are "broken" that you and your missional community could possibly take part in restoring as a display of the gospel. You'll discuss this together tomorrow. Here are some things you might notice: an elderly person's home or yard; a park or public space that needs some lovin'; A neighbor's fence; an alley or empty lot that is full of trash; kids with nowhere to go after school; people who seem lonely or discarded...

Identify two or three people or families in your neighborhood that do not know the gospel? How could you begin to speak the good news into their lives? How could you begin to serve them as a demonstration of the gospel? Write down some ideas.

Remember, it is this combined proclamation and demonstration of the gospel that is most powerful!

Find a way to share your weekly meal together out in the neighborhood or city. Some place simple, local and that allows for a little conversation. Discuss together...

Compare your notes from yesterday's Action:

What common things did you notice?

What things could be done that seem simple, only requiring some intentional action?

Which things would require some planning, resources and time to restore?

Which of these things could you restore together as a community?

Discipleship and living a "missional" life is ultimately about people. Who did you see or meet that you might invite into community with you, showing them what God is like?

Also, make plans to get together in the next week or two to actively demonstrate the restoration of the gospel through some project or service to others. Remember to look for ways to simultaneously proclaim the good news as you demonstrate it.

Talk about who in your group more naturally tends toward "demonstrating" the gospel and who tends more toward "proclaiming" the power of the gospel? Remember, we need each other and our different gifts and perspectives to have the fullest expression of the good news to our neighbors and friends!

The gospel is not just about my individual happiness or God's plan for my life.

It is about God's plan for the world.

Jesus helped clarify how we accomplish the ultimate "why" of the gospel—the restoration of all things—by giving us his mission: *"Go and make disciples"* (Matthew 28:19).

As the arts, industry, politics, families—all areas of culture—are increasingly filled with Jesus' disciples bringing about his gospel restoration, the earth is being filled with his glory. That is the point of the restoration of all things—that God would be glorified!

Discipleship is the only mission that Jesus gave his church. It is how the gospel goes out and multiplies and accomplishes the restoration of all things.

So how does this work?

Jesus said, *"If you hold to my teaching, you are really my disciples. Then you will know the truth, and the truth will set you free."*

Let's clarify what Jesus said here. He is saying that walking in his ways, obeying his teachings is what it means to be his disciple. And this is what will lead us to know the truth (gospel) and that truth will set us free.

Astounding. Did you notice the order here?

If a person lives as a disciple, walking in Jesus ways, *then* they will come to know the truth that sets them free!

Then I wonder why we have so often done things in the exact opposite order with people. We have traditionally thought that if a person believed what we told them about Jesus, they would get set free and then they could start getting "discipled."

But this is not what Jesus said, or how he modeled all of this. Jesus spent years with his disciples, none of whom were "Christians," leading them to walk in his ways and obey his teachings. Then, *over time,* they came to believe the truth about who he was and were set free.

This means that we are called to invite others to walk in the ways of Jesus with us as we are living our everyday lives as his disciples. We actually disciple others *to* Christ. This is how they will come to believe the gospel that we proclaim and demonstrate; by participating in his life and community where they can repeatedly see and hear the gospel as it comes into contact and contrast with their lives.

6.6 Notes

We are always in "discipleship mode." Others are either seeing us live our life as a servant, submitted to Jesus and focused on others, or they are seeing us serve our selves and build our own kingdom.

How does this idea of discipling a person to Christ change the way you see your time spent with others?

Who could you more intentionally invite to "walk in the ways of Jesus" with you in normal everyday life?

What regular parts of your day or week could easily be done with someone else that you are discipling? (Think about time you already spend doing things, but invite someone to do it with you.)

How different is this from the way you were discipled? When did this occur in your life: before or after your "conversion"?

6.7
ReCREATE

Jesus said, "Are you tired? Worn out? Burned out on religion? Come to me. Get away with me and you'll recover your life. I'll show you how to take a real rest. Walk with me and work with me—watch how I do it. Learn the unforced rhythms of grace. I won't lay anything heavy or ill-fitting on you. Keep company with me and you'll learn to live freely and lightly."

[Matthew 11:28-30 The Message]

Consider This

Our lives as disciples who make disciples should not be a burden. Life in Christ, living out of our recreated identity, should fill us with peace, joy and great contentment. If you are feeling that your Christian life, ministry or life in community is a heavy load, then it is not Jesus' load you are carrying. Rest in his completed work. It is Jesus who will make disciples of us all. We are only called to walk along with him in loving obedience.

WEEK 7
Gospel Identity

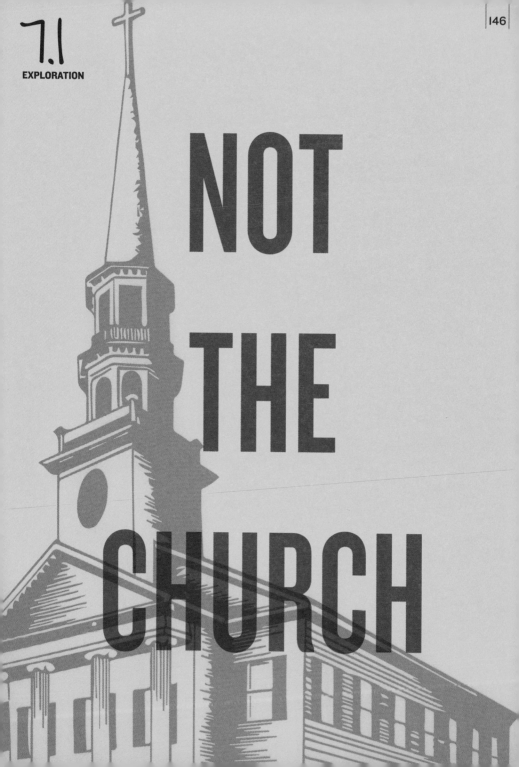

NOT THE CHURCH

Who Are You?

I spent a lot of time traveling in and out of South Sudan during the decades-long civil war that ravaged the nation and its people. I took part in different "missions" to deliver much needed food and life-saving medicine, encouraging the local Christians as we preached the gospel whenever we could. These experiences were life changing for me in so many ways. One of the biggest things that stuck out, and began to stick *to* me, was how different "church" was in Sudan compared to the life I was living as a Christian, father and pastor in the United States. It seemed that whenever I was over there in Africa with the Sudanese believers, we were the church.

Me and them.

We were the church.

They didn't have buildings or any resources to "do" church. No elaborate Sunday services with lights and sound systems. They just *were* the church. Loving each other, sharing what very, very little they had. Literally laying their lives down for the sake of the gospel. And these Christians (who owned nothing—no things) were so filled with JOY.

Seriously filled with joy!

We don't GO to church... we ARE the church!

The Sudanese Christians I spent time with had no possessions, no country, no homes and in some cases no earthly families— nothing left to put their hope in. But they had found the only thing that truly satisfies our hearts: Jesus. They didn't need material possessions to be happy. And there was nothing profound for them to do.

They had found their very life—their identity and purpose—in Jesus.

Jesus died that we might be restored to a right relationship with his Father, back into the family we were originally created to be a part of. It is Jesus who pursues, secures and maintains our position in the family of God.

It's all about Jesus.

And the Bible teaches that if we are in Christ, the gospel has made us part of a family of *missionary servants,* sent to serve the world as disciples who make disciples. This is who we are. This is our new gospel identity.

The more we understand and believe this to be true, the more our lives will be transformed. And the more peace, joy and purpose we will find in life.

So, who are you?

7.1 Notes

What are the things that you most regularly spend time doing as a family? (List at least six or seven.)

What are the things that you most regularly spend time doing at church or in your Christian life?

How different are these lists? Could/should these look more similar?

Do you primarily see the church as a family? What would it look like to live as disciples of Jesus who really believe that they are a family of missionary servants?

7.2
MEDITATION

We've learned that the reason for our salvation was to make us disciples of Jesus who make disciples, filling all things with the glory of God. Filling the world with Jesus. We are being re-created into a fuller, richer representation of the image of God, our true identity.

"And, I will be a Father to you, and you will be my **sons and daughters**," says the Lord Almighty.
[2 Corinthians 6:18]

Both the one who makes people holy and those who are made holy are **of the same family**. So Jesus is not ashamed to call them brothers and sisters.
[Hebrews 2:11]

In your relationships with one another, have the same mindset as Christ Jesus: Who, being in very nature God, did not consider equality with God something to be used to his own advantage; rather, he made himself nothing by taking the very nature of **a servant**....
[Philippians 2:5-7]

And whoever wants to be first must be your slave—just as the Son of Man did not come to be served, but **to serve, and to give his life** as a ransom for many.
[Matthew 20:27-28]

But you will receive power when the Holy Spirit comes on you; and you will be **my witnesses** in Jerusalem, and in all Judea and Samaria, and to the ends of the earth.
[Acts 1:8]

Again Jesus said, "Peace be with you! As the Father has sent me, **I am sending you**."
[John 20:21]

7.2 Notes

How often on your faith journey, and as a Christian, have you felt like it was up to you to remain close to God? Always.......Sometimes.......Never?

What changes in your heart when you think of God as your perfectly patient and loving Father who is pursuing you?

What do you think it means to "have the same mindset as Christ" in your relationships with others?

When you think about being a "slave" to someone else (Matthew 20:27-28), what comes to mind? How would you treat them...how would they view you? What happens in your heart as you consider this?

Look up Ephesians 1:3-14 and see what you've inherited as Jesus' brother or sister. List them below:

When you don't "feel like" serving others or speaking truth into a situation or living on mission, where do you go for strength and renewal?

How does knowing that you are now filled with the power that raised Christ from the dead (the Holy Spirit) change this perspective?

As disciples
of Jesus, we are...

family

servants

missionaries

Our New Identity

When Jesus gave us the privilege and call to make disciples and baptize them (Matthew 28:19), he was inviting us to help people find a new identity.

To become a Christian is to enter into a relationship with God as our Father, to find a new **family,** both eternally and right now!

Following the example of Jesus, the Son, we live as **servants** in the world. As he served, we too should serve.

Jesus sent his disciples into the world, promising that the Holy Spirit would lead them. We now have the same Spirit living within us, sending us as **missionaries** into every context of life.

He said, "As the Father has sent me, I am sending you." Our identity in Christ makes us **a family of missionary servants,** sent as disciples who make disciples!

We often hear Matthew 28:19 quoted as a part of a baptism ceremony. But we sometimes miss the full meaning. In one short statement, Jesus laid out the entire picture of this new identity that we have entered into:

"Therefore go and make disciples of all nations, baptizing them in the name of the Father and of the Son and of the Holy Spirit."

There it is.

Our baptism is not a magic spell or just some culturally ancient ritual; we are baptized, soaked, and established into a new identity within a new community—the church—and then given our mission and the means to accomplish it.

"Into the NAME OF the Father, and the NAME OF the Son, and the NAME OF the Holy Spirit...."

This is a huge identity statement. It's who we are **today!** As disciples, our identity comes from the fullness of our God who is three-in-one.

7.3 Notes

What would change in your life if you lived like a full-time missionary?

Where, what, who is your personal "mission field"?

Who specifically are you making disciples of in your community?

Who in your life seems to be open and "leaning in" to deeper relationship?

Who are the people that you seem naturally drawn to when you think about sharing your faith?

How much of a servant are you? How would taking on the posture of a servant change the way you interact with the following people (Be specific, list a couple of ideas next to each on how you could increasingly live out of your identity as a servant):

Friends?

Parents?

Spouse? (if you are married)

Children?

Neighbors?

Co-workers?

How/why is serving others such a strong display of gospel good news?

7.4
ACTION

Often we fail to live out our new identity because we don't pray and plan in advance, bringing a new level of intentionality to our lives. Today we want to make some plans to live out of our missionary identity with greater gospel-intentionality. Pray and ask the Spirit to give you ideas about who you could have a meal with next week; just one out of the 21 or so meals that you will probably have.

Who seems to be "leaning in" relationally toward your life, and possibly, faith? Write down at least three or four names and give one person (or couple) a call and invite them to share a meal next week on (or before) your Action Day. It is important to pray about this and do this today so that you'll give people enough time to schedule this. Keep calling folks until something lines up; trust the Holy Spirit to work things out! You'll find that even those who are not available will be blessed by your invitation.

Suggestions
You may want to pair up with another person or couple in your group and co-host this meal.

This meal could be a lunch or dinner...or breakfast for that matter!

Ask the person you invite what their favorite foods are or if they have any food allergies.

Host this meal in a home, not a restaurant, so you can share your life and have good conversations without feeling awkward.

Try to eliminate as many distractions as you can during this meal so you can focus on your guests.

Note: **Be sure to have this meal before your Community Day next week. You are going to be getting together as a group to share what you learned and experienced.**

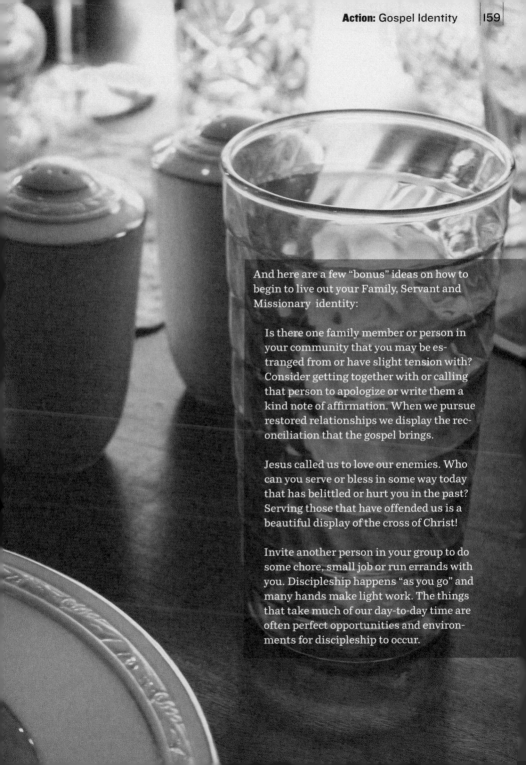

And here are a few "bonus" ideas on how to begin to live out your Family, Servant and Missionary identity:

Is there one family member or person in your community that you may be estranged from or have slight tension with? Consider getting together with or calling that person to apologize or write them a kind note of affirmation. When we pursue restored relationships we display the reconciliation that the gospel brings.

Jesus called us to love our enemies. Who can you serve or bless in some way today that has belittled or hurt you in the past? Serving those that have offended us is a beautiful display of the cross of Christ!

Invite another person in your group to do some chore, small job or run errands with you. Discipleship happens "as you go" and many hands make light work. The things that take much of our day-to-day time are often perfect opportunities and environments for discipleship to occur.

7.5
COMMUNITY

Gospel, Community, and Mission

Everything we've looked at this week has shown us our new gospel identity. Have you noticed that this is not only an individual reality, but a communal one as well? In fact, Jesus never intended his disciples to go and live out a personal faith on a personal mission all alone.

Our identity in Christ is an identity best understood and expressed in community. It is when we live and work together in a bond of love and unity that all the parts of Jesus' body (the church) come together into a glorious display of what he is like.

In fact, we cannot become mature disciples of Jesus apart from of a gospel-centered community that is living life on mission. That's because a community that does not have the gospel as its center and purpose is just another group or club. And it's when we really live on Jesus' mission that our true need for him and the gospel comes out in greater ways.

The Holy Spirit uses these experiences and the various parts of the body in our community to help conform us to Christ.

This is how true discipleship happens. Not in a classroom, but in a family of missionary servants.

Today, let's focus on linking two aspects of our identity: Family and Servant.

In what ways over the next few weeks, and in the months ahead, could you begin to tangibly live as family together…treating each other as brothers and sisters? (Maybe revisit your thoughts from 7.1) Be creative, but realistic. The goal as a missional community is to increasingly, over time, begin to live more like a family; sharing resources, time, burdens… doing *life together*.

Healthy families serve each other in selfless and sometimes sacrificial ways. How could you begin to authentically serve one another as you move forward together in community? Look for "pain points" in your lives and areas where you can lighten each other's load.

By the way, other's outside your community will be blown away that you live this way—a great display of the gospel!

WE CANNOT BECOME MATURE DISCIPLES OF JESUS APART FROM A GOSPEL-CENTERED COMMUNITY THAT IS LIVING LIFE ON MISSION.

do

does not equal

be

The way of the world is this: we do things (perform, serve, work) to have value in the eyes of our family, friends, parents, spouse, siblings, boss, pastor, etc. If we do a good enough job and are perceived as valuable, then people will want us around. We'll feel desirable. Out of this activity we often form our identity. What we DO has led to who we ARE. Or at least we think it has. There is a huge problem with this: it is terribly dangerous, it eventually crushes us, and it goes against how God sees us.

If we are followers of Christ, we are not who we once were, but have truly been made new creations in Christ. This is part of God's restoration of all things, and it includes us—*now.*

Our identity in Christ leads us to live in new ways. We'll look closely at the everyday stuff of life next week, but for now, as we contemplate living in community as a family of missionary servants, our human tendency is to think about all the stuff we need to start DOing and forget that this is more about our *BEing.*

A bird is not a bird because it can fly; it flies because it is a bird. Fish swim because they get to, not to prove they're fish and please the other fish.

It is the same with our new gospel identity. We will live in new ways and do different things as Christians because we are new people. A recreated and restored humanity. As the gospel recreates our hearts, our lives follow.

Don't believe the DO = BE lies anymore.

7.6 Notes

Finish these sentences in light of God's love. (Take your time. The fuller your answer, the deeper this will begin to sink into your heart.)

Before Christ, my identity and self-worth was most shaped by...

Now, because of the gospel I am...

As a Christian, I thought these things were important in order to please God...

Now I know Jesus did everything that was needed to pay for my sin and secure the Father's acceptance on my behalf, so I can...

How amazing to think that we are now part of the family of our eternal God!

As a child of God I never have to...

As a child of God I can always...

List some truths that come to mind about your life because of your new gospel identity...

7.7

ReCREATE

Since we believe that Christ died for all, we also believe that we have all died to our old life. He died for everyone so that those who receive his new life will no longer live for themselves. Instead, they will live for Christ, who died and was raised for them.

So we have stopped evaluating others from a human point of view. At one time we thought of Christ merely from a human point of view. How differently we know him now! This means that anyone who belongs to Christ has become a new person. The old life is gone; a new life has begun!

And all of this is a gift from God, who brought us back to himself through Christ. And God has given us this task of reconciling people to him.

(2 Corinthians 5:14-18 NLT)

Consider This

It is Jesus who died to free us from our old life of sin and self. It is Jesus who now lives in us by his Spirit. He has given us the awesome privilege of partnering with him to bring others back to God.

All of this is a gift, not a burden. We don't have to work for God—we get to work with him, under his power and strength, showing the world what he is like.

It is critical to remember that our Father in heaven loves and accepts us exactly the same if we are out doing "missional stuff" or not. We are not loved because of what WE do; we are loved because of what JESUS did! This great love shown to us motivates us to live in ways that reflect God's character and identity, now imparted to us.

WEEK 8

Gospel Rhythms

8.1

EXPLORATION

How We Live

Over the past several weeks we have learned a lot about the gospel, how it affects all of life and even how to begin to listen to others and speak the good news into their lives.

But if you're like me, I have a hard time effectively translating what I am learning about God and the gospel into everyday life. How do I more consistently live out my gospel identity (a family of missionary servants) at home, at work and in community? It's normal to feel some tension related to living on mission; you have been living in certain patterns for years and it isn't always immediately clear how to live this out in your day-to-day life.

Here are six **rhythms of life** that are happening in every context and culture. I have found that these "rhythms" (all of which are a picture of the gospel) help me to see all the normal routines of life as easy opportunities for living out my gospel identity and inviting others to life in Christ. They have given me "handles" to hold on to without becoming a missional to-do list.

In many ways, you are already living in these rhythms and may not have noticed. Take a look and think about what they might mean for you as a part of your daily and weekly rhythm of life.

Note: It might be helpful to post these someplace you'll often see them (the refrigerator or the bathroom mirror) to help you "re-rhythm" your life and to remind you of easy, daily opportunities to live out your gospel identity.

Know the Story

Everyone has a story to tell (or many); we are a story-formed people. Make it a habit to get to know the stories of the people in your life and community. They are dying to tell you! Help others see how their stories intersect and mirror God's story. In order to grow in this ability you will need to get more and more familiar with the the story of God.

Listen

God is waiting to talk with us. Set aside regular times to just listen to God. Try having times of prayer where all you do is listen for the voice of God to speak, resisting the urge to give God your to-do list. Regularly practice listening "backward" by spending time in God's Word. And actively listen "forward" to hear what God is saying to you today through his Spirit and through your community.

Celebrate

Gather consistently throughout the week with your community to share stories and celebrate all that God is doing in and amongst you. Invite others to these celebrations as a way of displaying God's extravagant blessings.

Bless

Intentionally bless others through words, gifts or actions. God desires that all nations—all people—would be blessed through Jesus. Seek God's direction for who he would have you tangibly bless each week.

Eat

Regularly eat meals with others as a reminder of our common need for God and his faithfulness to provide both physically and spiritually. Start by consistently having at least one meal each week with a sojourner (a not-yet-believer) enjoying the meal with you.

ReCreate

Take time each week to rest, play, create, and restore beauty in ways that display the gospel, resting in Jesus' completed work on our behalf. Cultivate this gospel rhythm of rest and create—ReCreate—in your life. This is truly what it means to "keep the sabbath."

8.1 Notes

Which of the "rhythms" jumped out at as most appealing to you? Which stuck out as hardest to engage in? Why?

In what ways are you already living within in these rhythms? Write down even the obvious ones...

How could you bring greater gospel intentionality to each of these rhythms?

How much of your prayer times are spent just listening for God to speak to you? Is this a part of your regular prayer rhythm? Why or why not?

In what ways do you practice the "ReCreate" rhythm?

Do you have a regular time of sabbath? What does that most often look like? If not, how can you start?

8.2

MEDITATION

The Rhythms

With many stories like these, he (Jesus) presented his message to them, fitting the stories to their experience and maturity. He was never without a story when he spoke. When he was alone with his disciples, he went over everything, sorting out the tangles, untying the knots. (Mark 4:33–34 The Message)

As often as possible Jesus withdrew to out-of-the-way places for prayer. (Luke 5:16 The Message)

So Jesus said, "When you have lifted up the Son of Man, then you will know that I am he and that I do nothing on my own but speak just what the Father has taught me." (John 8:28 The Message)

Every year Jesus parents traveled to Jerusalem for the Feast of Passover. When he was twelve years old, they went up as they always did for the Feast. (Luke 2:41 The Message)

When the Passover Feast, celebrated each spring by the Jews,
was about to take place, Jesus traveled up to Jerusalem.
(John 2:13 The Message)

of Jesus' Life

That evening, after the sun was down, they brought sick and
evil-afflicted people to him, the whole city lined up at his
door He cured their sick bodies and tormented spirits.
(Mark 1:34 The Message)

The Son of Man came eating and drinking, and you say, "Here
is a glutton and a drunkard, a friend of tax collectors and
sinners." (Luke 7:34 The Message)

He said to the man with the crippled hand, "Stand here where
we can see you." Then he spoke to the people: "What kind of
action suits the Sabbath best? Doing good or doing evil?
Helping people or leaving them helpless?" No one said a
word. (Mark 3:3-4 The Message)

8.2 Notes

Often the ways in which Jesus lived were misunderstood. Why do you think this was?

Which rhythms of your life are most in line with the story of God and his original plans for how we should live? Think back to our Human Job Description on Day 2.3.

Which rhythms of your life are least in line with God's story?

How do you think people in your life and community would react to you living a life increasingly shaped by your gospel identity in each of these six rhythms? How would their views of God begin to change?

Additional.

Nick and Sarah both grew up going to church with their families. They have been part of a large local church since a year after they got married, and have worked hard to raise their kids to know God and love others.

Recently some friends invited them to be a part of a missional community that is forming in their neighborhood. Nick found that he is more excited about his faith than he has been in years. He had always felt that there had to be more to Christianity than his weekly visit to church on Sunday and the Bible study he and Sarah led in their home. For years, Sarah had been going on "missions trips" to Haiti and wondered why they couldn't just live like missionaries back at home—every day—in their neighborhood and city.

The leaders of their missional community have been challenging them to live as a family of missionary servants, increas-

ingly reorienting their lives around those they are trying to reach with the gospel and disciple in their faith. They are loving all of this...

But.

Their lives already seem so busy with work, three kids, soccer practices, caring for Nick's aging mother and all the other normal stuff of life. Most days they both go to bed tired and praying for strength to make it to the weekend. How will they ever possibly add more to their busy schedules?

They really do believe that the Bible teaches that Jesus' disciples are called and sent to make disciples as a way of life. But their lives already seem so full with family and Christian friends, not to mention serving at the church. How does someone actually live this missional life in the world today?

Intentional.

I want to suggest that the secret to increasingly living our lives on mission is to move from seeing a gospel-centered mission as something "additional" that needs to be tacked on to life, to seeing all the normal stuff and rhythms of life as full of opportunity for the gospel. We need only to fill them with greater gospel intentionality. We must move from an *additional mindset* to an *intentional mindset* in the normal rhythms of life that God has given us.

"Be very careful, then, how you live—not as unwise but as wise, making the most of every opportunity, because the days are evil." (Ephesians 5:15-16)

We only have one life to live. If we are determined to live out our "American Dream" version of life while attempting to add in God's version of life at the same time, it will never work. This is what leads many to burnout and frustration in their Christian life.

B.3 Notes

Here are several areas of life that most of us already have and can easily live with gospel intentionality:

Daily meals
Most of us already eat 21 (or more) meals each week.

5 days of work each week
Can you believe you actually get paid to be a full-time missionary!?

Regular trips to the same cafe, store or restaurant
Do you know the stories of any of the staff or regulars?

Yard work and home maintenance
There are many young men that would love to learn how to lead a family and care for a home!

Trips to the grocery store or park
A great time to spend with younger friends who do not have your skills in these areas.

Hours in the car commuting or running errands
Built-in times to spend listening to God.

Countless soccer games and PTA meetings
Daily or weekly opportunities to treat others as family

Life in an apartment building or dorm room
Built-in density of potential relationships.

What keeps you from living with greater gospel intentionality within the rhythm of things that you are already doing?

Which of the suggestions on the previous page could you begin to engage in immediately?

How much easier and more appealing is it to consider living with greater gospel intentionality as part of a community instead of going it alone?

A Simple Meal

Your prayers and plans from last week should lead you to have a meal today (or perhaps earlier this week) with a friend or two who don't follow Jesus. Remember, this time of eating together is an opportunity to live in normal, daily rhythms while displaying God's generosity, creativity and care. God is the ultimate provider for all of our needs...that is why this is a picture of the gospel.

Relax.

Have fun.

Be yourself!

As you engage in conversation ask them to tell you a little bit of their stories. Listen for the themes of creation, fall, redemption, restoration as they speak. What is the good news to them? If natural and unforced, you may be able to share, from memory, your own gospel story that you wrote in Week 3.

Think through the other rhythms and see how many you can naturally engage in during just one meal.

Write down some of your observations...surprises...praises!

8.5
COMMUNITY

This week, in the Rhythm of *Celebration,* go out to a cool restaurant or find a fun place to have a picnic and enjoy one another as you work through the following reflections...

How did your meals go this week with your un-believing friends?

What common themes came up?

What emotions were you feeling before having this dinner? What emotions did you experience after?

What did you learn from having this dinner? Did you get to know their stories?

Based on their unique story, how might you bless this person in the immediate future?

Did anything happen that surprised you or that you are praising God for?

How could you naturally follow up relationally with these folks, perhaps as a community?

What would it look like to make this "gospel-eating" a normal rhythm of your life as a community?

If anyone in your group did not have someone over for dinner this week, ask them to share why. What were their obstacles? Discuss how the 4 G's (the Four Eternal

Truths) might reveal an opportunity for transformation and obedience. Be gentle, but don't fear holding each other accountable in love.

Additional questions to discuss as you finish up this primer experience together...

How have you grown in "gospel fluency" over these past 8 weeks?

What has been most effective in shaping you to be able to bring the gospel to bear on issues in your life and others' lives?

How and when are you beginning to speak the gospel to others in your life?

How has your understanding of your new identity in Christ begun to change how you see and live:

In your relationship with God?
With your family?
Those at work?
In dealing with sin in your life?
In how you prioritize your time and resources?

Closing thoughts...

Be sure to spend some time truly celebrating the big "wins" and heart/life-level changes you've experienced over the past 8 weeks. Thank God together for this journey.

Hopefully now, you've got the idea of how to make these rhythms more natural. A good way to move forward is to simply keep going!

As you now wake up daily to look for Creation ➡ Fall ➡ Redemption ➡ Restoration, make a commitment to revisit Day 6.4 and find a way this next week to bring some redemption and restoration to something you noticed wasn't as God intended it. Remember, sometimes bringing redemption and restoration is as easy as picking up a bit of trash or dropping by to visit a lonely neighbor.

Let this experience be a reminder to you but also the beginning of new gospel rhythms for you.

8.6

CALIBRATION

Baby Steps (on Steroids!)

Ok, there's even more good news about all of this. We are not made new creations, given a new identity, and then shoved out the door and told to go and live this out under our own strength, power and wisdom. God does not expect us to suddenly become perfect super-Christians (always wise, always gentle, always loving) overnight. The Bible compares this new life to taking a walk. One step at a time, each new area of trust in God is connected to the next one on a journey.

And the best part is that we are now filled with a new eternal, God-sized power supply.

For most of my early life as a Christian, I never picked up on the reality that Jesus' earthly years of ministry were completely guided by the Holy Spirit. I had always thought, "Well, Jesus is both God and man, so he knows what's up and just does everything perfectly, naturally." Well sort of. It's true that Jesus is both God and man and he lived his life without ever sinning. But as a human, like you and me, he fully submitted to and was guided by the Spirit. His life is a picture of the perfect work of the Holy Spirit in man.

Jesus was born by the work of the Spirit.
(Luke 1:35)

Jesus was led by the Spirit to suffer temptation and come out spotless.
(Luke 4:1-2)

Jesus was empowered by the Spirit to do the ministry he did.
(Matthew 12:28; Acts 10:38)

Jesus was full of wisdom and knowledge by the Holy Spirit.
(Isaiah 11:2-3)

Jesus spoke only the words given him by the Spirit.
(John 3:34; 8:28)

Jesus was raised from the dead by the power of the Spirit.
(Romans 8:11)

Wouldn't it be great if we had this same Spirit living inside of us guiding, empowering, and giving us words to say (or not say)? Oh wait...!

We do.

8.6 Notes

What's Next?

Write a short letter to the Holy Spirit. Tell him what you are most concerned about in your life today. Tell him what challenges you are facing in your heart concerning living out your gospel identity on mission. Tell him about the people in your life that you are praying would come to know Jesus as Lord and Savior.

Then ask him to show you the first step he wants you to take in this area or with a certain individual. Just ask, "what's next?" Then listen. He'll speak, I promise you. Ask him to give you the strength to be obedient and do what he tells you. God always provides for what he commands. Trust him with this.

Then do it again...and again...until listening to the Spirit and doing what he says becomes a rhythm in your life.

Jesus said, "Surely I am with you always, to the very end of the age."

[Matthew 28:20]

The Israelites were a special people, a kingdom of priests set apart to show the world what God is like. He promised to lead them to a land flowing with milk and honey, which is a way of saying it was an awesome place filled with opportunity and blessing!

The people had God's promises, but they lacked faith and were afraid to enter the land and claim his abundant provision.

This promise of blessing for God's chosen people, the Church, still stands today. The writer of Hebrews reminds us:

"Therefore, since the promise of entering his rest still stands, let us be careful that none of you be found to have fallen short of it. For we also have had the good news proclaimed to us, just as they did; but the message they heard was of no value to them, because they did not share the faith of those who obeyed." (Hebrews 4:1-2)

Consider This...
Today, the same as it has always been, God is calling us to a life of faith and trust in relationship with him. He is not sending us out to accomplish his mission and live in his ways under our own strength and protection. He goes with us. His Spirit guides us into all truth, comforting us and strengthening us for this adventure as his family of missionary servants!

Epilogue and Appendix

In Closing

The Gospel Primer:
In Closing

You Made It!

We've learned a lot together over the past 8 weeks, and hopefully you are feeling more confident in your understanding of the gospel and how to naturally speak the good news to each other inside and outside our Christian community. Like we've said all along the journey, this new "gospel fluency" is like anything else—it needs to be practiced, often.

As a kid, I loved watching the Wizard of Oz. It came on television once a year and like clockwork my family would make enormous amounts of popcorn, pull out gallons of soda pop and all line up on blankets on the floor to watch in amazement. My favorite part of the movie (other than when the Wicked Witch gets water thrown on her and melts down to nothing under her big black witch hat) was when the movie went from black and white to living, luscious, dripping color! I would wait for that part. Everything seemed to explode with life after that.

All of this information on the gospel is similar in that it needs to be lived out over and over in everyday life for it to move from black and white (like words on a page) to bold, vivid, 3-D color! You need to continue to experience the gospel in an incarnational community and live as a full-color display of the gospel for others to see.

Some of you have taken the time to not only go through the *Gospel Primer* as a group, but you have gone through our other primers as well. But whether or not you are just getting started as a community or have been at it for a while, I want to strongly urge you to begin to move past this into living a more intuitive, gospel-centered lifestyle. You have the Spirit of God living in you! You have access to the very life of Christ at all times!

Remember, this is not about how well we speak or how perfect our lives look. We are called to live in a trusting, Spirit-guided relationship with God where he takes the lead and uses us to bless others and bring glory to himself. It is time to move beyond 8 week studies and get on the faith train!

As I travel from city to city, country to country spending time with believers and not-yet believers from all over the world, I have noticed something strikingly similar. Nearly all the Christians I talk to about living an intuitive and gospel-centered life in community say something like, "Yeah, I would LOVE that, and it probably works where you live, but here in my neighborhood, or in my city, or in this country...or in our denomination...this would never happen."

I hope you won't limit God or predetermine in your hearts what will or won't happen. What makes the gospel so miraculous is that it HAS worked and will always show fruit when humble friends share this great story. When someone puts their faith and their lives in God's hands, it is the greatest miracle of all. Will all your friends respond? No. But if even one does, it will be worth all the effort, prayer, and time you give them.

I'll be praying that you will be part of a community that will believe what you have heard and actually go and live out the gospel, by the power of the Holy Spirit.

I hope to run into you some day, doing all the normal stuff of life, with a bunch of disciples in tow and the gospel just dripping out of your mouths and being proclaimed in every step, bite of food and breath you take.

Your brother and servant,
Caesar

The Gospel Primer:
Sample Gospel Stories

Kristy's Story

I am the oldest of five kids in my family. I have a younger brother and three younger sisters. We're all pretty close and get along, I guess. My father was in the military so we moved around a lot. We moved eight times between kindergarten and seventh grade. I learned how to make friends pretty quickly, but I was always worried about being the "new kid" and what people thought about me. I wasn't very athletic, so I never fit in with the sports-jock kids. I ended up listening to a lot of music and hanging out around any of the local musicians I could find. I really wanted to fit in with them and find a set of friends who would just accept me for who I was.

Because I wasn't very close with my Dad, I ended up looking for acceptance from most of the boys I met. Most of them seemed to reject me or were only interested in one thing—seeing what they could "get off of me." I never felt attractive, so I tried to "dress to impress" and show off what little physical assets I thought I had. I also started to give myself away physically—in little ways at first—making out and going "too far." I did whatever it took to keep a boy's attention and keep him calling me back. Eventually I talked myself into believing that guy after guy really cared about me, and I started having sex with some of them. The crazy thing was, that after I had sex with them, they usually disappeared and rejected me, which only made me feel worse. Then I would try harder to find love and acceptance.

When we were moving around the country growing up, I would often attend church with my new neighbors, or spend the summers going to vacation bible school. I really liked those times and remember thinking, "I do believe in God and wish I knew him better." I learned a lot about God. I remember learning that God loved me, and that he wanted me to save sex for marriage. It was not pleasing to God for me to have sex before marriage because I belonged to him, he loved me and had a more perfect plan for my life. That sounded awesome, but I still wanted to be loved now—today—by someone here, for who I was. I seemed to try anything and everything on my own to get that love.

After I left high school, our family moved back to Washington. I met up with some old friends I had known really well from grade school. They seemed to accept me and be interested in ME—who I was today. Even some of the cute guys were cool to me, and they weren't trying to get me to sleep with them. My friend Emily was so helpful. One night we stayed up really late at her house and talked until four in the morning. I told her everything that had been going on in my life and how awful I felt inside because of how I had given myself away for years to guys who never cared for me. I also told her I was starting to feel pretty guilty with God about all of this.

Emily was a Christian and had been since I met her years ago. She told me that night that she loved me and so did God. She told me that God loved me enough to send Jesus to earth on a rescue mission to show me God's love. I told her, "I know that, but that was so long ago and I have done all these things that are wrong. I feel like God is probably angry at me, and that I will never be loved or find a guy to marry and love me."

Emily said, "You are looking for a perfect guy. One who will love you—skinny or fat, smart or silly. A guy who will never leave you or find another woman he loves more. That guy is Jesus. He is the only perfect man that ever lived, and he does love you, Kristy. All those years of trying to find acceptance and giving yourself away to boys was sinful. It hurts, and it has separated you from a closer relationship with God. But Jesus came to show you his love by giving his life on the cross to pay the penalty for all of your sins. God has accepted his sacrifice in place of our sins. If you believe this, Kristy, and trust Jesus with your life, you can have the love and relationship you have always wanted—with Jesus, who is the perfect guy! Nothing you have done or can do will ever cause Jesus to love you any more or any less. He already died in your place and wants you to trust him...do you trust Jesus, Kristy?"

I really wanted to. My heart broke that night, and Emily helped me tell Jesus everything I was feeling in a prayer. I asked him to forgive me, love me and help me live in a new way. Emily assured me that I was forgiven, and now Jesus would live with me, love me and give me a new life if I continued to trust him.

In the last year everything has begun to change for me. I still don't have a steady boyfriend, but I am beginning to feel like Jesus is so much more important to me than any guy could ever be. I am learning that when I feel ugly or stupid that God does not see me that way. I am a new person now—a daughter of God's who was rescued and is loved by Jesus. AMAZING! ME??? That gives me a lot of strength when I need it. God has been re-writing my story. I am finding new friends that also love God and have been rescued by Jesus, and these friends accept me for who I am right now. They are showing me God's love in person, and it's pretty cool. I don't know everything about God or the Bible, but I want everyone to know that they don't have to try and prove themselves or be someone they're not in order to be loved. God loves them!

When I look back at the person I was over the past few years—giving myself away to find love...Thank God that I AM LOVED and don't have to do ANYTHING for his love. That is so amazing!

Nate's Story

I'm not sure how to tell you about my life... it's kind of crazy to me too. After years of being a normal kid—going to school, trying hard to get good grades, going to church and youth group—I started playing music. Guitar, actually. It made me feel awesome. Important. Alive. Like I had something special to give, you know? I decided I wanted to become a "rock star" as a career. Can you do that??? I was going to be a rock star instead of an electrical engineer like my dad wanted. I have three sisters—two older, one younger—and my dad always wanted me to have a "reliable job" like the one he's had for the last 30+ years. Yikes! I could never do that.

Everything started to be focused on music and image. I became pretty good at playing the guitar, but not like some sort of virtuoso really, just above average. But I loved it. I started to fall into everything that the rock and roll lifestyle seemed to promise. I started smoking marijuana and drinking because everyone else I hung out with did and expected me to, too—have to live up to the image, you know. But all the time I was still this guy who believed what I grew up learning in church. That was kind of weird, but I did believe that Jesus was God and that he came to earth to die for our sins. In fact, I could be hammered drunk at a party and tell you this stuff about how cool God really was. But none of this "head knowledge" or belief really made any difference in my life. I pretty much did whatever I wanted to do. I was just like Adam and Eve in the Bible, trying to manage the knowledge of right or wrong—good and evil—for myself. I wanted to rule my own life, you know? The only problem was, my life was going nowhere, and deep down inside I knew it. My life started coming apart, and my family was freaking out. I had little to do with all of my old "church friends." I guess I was just feeling guilty about my choices and behavior, even though it all seemed pretty cool to me still...sort of...

I started hanging out with Steve, another guitar player I knew and a few other people he hung out with (one girl was totally hot and I really liked her). I started to let my guard down—be my real self around them. They were really cool—these people said they loved Jesus—and I felt ease around them. They knew my dreams of becoming a professional musician, and they always came to see me play whenever I did a show or anything. They didn't seem that impressed with me, but kind of just loved me, you know? I really needed that... wanted that.

One of Steve's friends named Jason told me a story one night. It was from olden times and was about kings and kingdoms. He told me how awesome it was to live in a kingdom, back in the day, and to be loved, protected and taken care of by a king. He said that if you lived inside a kingdom back then, you were super thankful, because outside the kingdom walls was war, fighting and starvation, and everyone had to fend for themselves. But living under the rule and protection of the king was awesome because the king took care of you, protected you and met all of your needs.

Jason said that if you lived in those times, and lived within the kingdom, you would be stoked and wake up in the morning thankful, wondering, "How could I ever repay this king for all that he has done for me? He has saved me, protected me and meets all my needs." You would work really hard at any job that the king would give you in his kingdom because you were so thankful and wanted to show the king your love in return.

He told me that this is how Jesus is as our King. And that he wants to save us—he loves us and protects us, and he wants us to live our lives for him now. Not that we have to prove anything or repay him, but that he hopes our love for him would lead us to ask: "How could I live my life to show this King how much I love him and how thankful I am?" When Jason told me that story I asked Steve what he thought and what I should do. Steve said that he really loved that story and it was true. Jesus had come to save us from our self and sinful lives, and to protect us and give us life in his kingdom. That is what he wants for us.

I asked him, "If I believe this, will I have to give up playing in bands and pursuing music?" Steve said he didn't know, but God probably gave me this talent as a way of serving him in his kingdom. I needed to ask God that question. Right then I seemed to understand everything differently. God really DID love me, has made me, and has given me these talents and desires, but he wants to save me for himself and have me use my talents for him—to make him famous, not myself.

As crazy as it sounds, that day I asked God to forgive me for trying to live my life only for my own fame and fortune. I asked him to show me how to love him and use my life in any way he wanted. I was a little scared by all of this because I really loved music and was afraid I might end up a Jesus freak or something. But I had a sense of peace and trust, so I sort of "let go" of my dreams and plans and asked God to reshape them. Yikes!

I'm still playing guitar now—in fact I am in three different bands. One of them is a band with some other Christians I know, which is actually really cool. I'm learning a lot. My own band is made up of me, another Christian and two other guys that are not yet believers in Jesus. God has been teaching me a lot about myself through these two guys, which is making me love them. I really want them to come to understand our King Jesus and how much he loves them too. I am asking God to show me how to do this and explain all of this to them. My relationship with my family is a lot better now (even though my folks still wish I had a "real career"). Instead of trying to hide a bunch of stuff in my life from them, I am now able to live openly and real with them—so much easier!

I am still anxious to see how God uses these talents and desires He gave me...I am just glad that I am now "off the throne" and the King is in charge!

The Gospel Primer:
Footnotes

[1]**Page 2**
Keller, Tim. *Doing Justice.* Resurgence Conference. Seattle. (2006).
http://bit.ly/keller-dj

[2]**Page 98**
This powerful idea that all sin in our life comes from not believing one of these four eternal truths about God comes from Tim Chester and his book *You Can Change.* This has been a life-changing tool and way to speak the gospel into my life and my community. Many of my thoughts in this week have come from conversations I've been blessed to have with Tim. I could not more highly recommend that you read his book and dig a whole lot deeper into this gospel truth. Thanks Tim!

You Can Change: God's Transforming Power for Our Sinful Behavior and Negative Emotions, Crossway Books ISBN-10: 1433512319 / ISBN-13: 978-1433512315

[3]**Page 115**
This is adapted from Tim Keller, *Preaching to the Heart.*

Resources by Missio and Missio Publishing

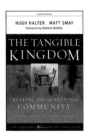

The story of *Missio* is described in detail in **The Tangible Kingdom: Creating Incarnational Community** by Hugh Halter and Matt Smay. The book has a companion guide called the **Tangible Kingdom Primer** which is designed to help Christians, churches, and small groups get on the pathway of spiritual formation and missional engagement. The primer creates opportunities to experience authentic missional community. It leads participants on a challenging 8-week journey toward an incarnational lifestyle and moves far beyond the typical small group experience.

Brandon Hatmaker's book **Barefoot Church** and the corresponding resource the **Barefoot Church Primer** tell the next chapter in the *Missio* story. The **Barefoot Church Primer** provides practical steps toward living out the good news of Jesus in a world full of need. The primer creates a unique opportunity to invite Christians from all backgrounds as well as non-Christian friends to join you in serving the least. The 8-week study works to naturally create a wealth of missional ministry openings as an outcome of learning to serve the least together.

In addition to these two books and the two corresponding primers, *Missio* develops training and resources to help your church take a more systematic approach to engaging in community and mission. The book **AND: The Gathered and Scattered Church** is written to help pastors guide churches into a more balanced and more missional mindset. The *Missio* website has many other resources, with more on the way, to help leaders cast vision and begin recruiting people to pilot incarnational communities. Visit *www. missio.us* for more information about our training and other resources.

Missio Publishing is committed to resourcing the church with practical tools to help it engage more effectively in missional and incarnational ministry. To purchase the primers and other resources, along with bulk discounts for churches, visit *www.missiopublishing.com.*